Some of the Story of 514 Squadron

Lancasters at Waterbeach

Some of the Story of 514 Squadron

Lancasters at Waterbeach

Harry Dison

**Bomber Command Books from
Mention the War**

First published in 1999 by Harry Dison. This edition first published in the United Kingdom 2015 by Mention the War Ltd.

The 514 Squadron badge is used and reproduced under licence from the MOD. Cover design: Topics - The Creative Partnership www.topicsdesign.co.uk

A CIP catalogue reference for this book is available from the British Library.

ISBN-13: 978-0993336089
ISBN-10: 0993336089

514 SQUADRON, R.A.F., WATERBEACH, 1944

This work is dedicated to Hugh Woodcraft.

Hugh restarted 514 Squadron Association in 1988
and managed it until 2000.

Other Bomber Command books from Mention the War

Striking Through Clouds – The War Diary of 514 Squadron RAF
(Simon Hepworth and Andrew Porrelli)

Nothing Can Stop Us – The Definitive History of 514 Squadron RAF
(Simon Hepworth, Andrew Porrelli and Harry Dison)

A Short War – The History of 623 Squadron RAF
(Steve Smith)

RAF Bomber Command Profiles: 617 Squadron
(Chris Ward)

Beach Boys and Bombers – The Aircrew of 514 Squadron (June 2016)
(Simon Hepworth, Andrew Porrelli and Roger Guernon)

The above books are available through Amazon in print, Kindle and, eventually, audio book format. For further details or to purchase a signed and dedicated copy, please contact *bombercommandbooks@gmail.com*

Table of Contents

Acknowledgements

To all who sent in contributions. Also for the special help and support from:

Clive Hill

Fred Brown

Hugh Woodcraft

'Mel' Melluish

David Oxton – Graphics

And especially my wife Mavis.

All original letters and other material submitted for possible inclusion in this work have been presented to the Waterbeach Military Heritage Museum for archive purposes.

Introduction

This work followed from a discussion with Hugh Woodcraft at the Reunion in 1998 and is mainly a compilation of written memories, or extracts from written memories, submitted in response to a circular letter sent to known Squadron members in November of that year. Many of these accounts were written in reply to the circular and some had been drafted for other reasons at earlier dates. Some official records and other data and information have also been incorporated to give a more complete picture of the Squadron. Accounts of aircrews naturally predominate, but mindful of the long hours of devoted work by ground crews and other supporting personnel, without whom the aircrews would never have left the ground, I am grateful for their few, but very valuable, contributions.

It is well over fifty years since the end of WWII and the disbanding of the Squadron, rather late in the day for compiling the 'story' but better late than never. I undertook the task with some trepidation, worried about the amount of work it would entail. However it has proved a fascinating experience to read the personal accounts and to discover so much about the Squadron that I did not know before. It was only when typing out the names of those who were killed in service with the Squadron that I fully realised the extent of such loss. It is gratifying to know that they are commemorated by the Plaque and the Book of Remembrance in Waterbeach Church and will not be forgotten.

The title 'Some Of The Story' was chosen because it is already too late for many of the young men and women who busily led their lives on the Squadron's airfields, although getting 'the chop' in '44 or in later years cannot alter the fact that the 'full story' could never have been told anyway.

I hope that there will be sufficient of the story here to convey to future readers, including descendants of those who served on the Squadron, some of the atmosphere and feeling of what it was like on one of the wartime Bomber Airfields.

Harry Dison

About the Author

Christened Henry Burrows Dison (always Harry), I was born in Liverpool in May 1925. Aged 14 when war was declared, I became an evacuee when the technical college I attended went to Shrewsbury. The first six or seven months of the war was known as the 'phoney war', as little happened in the west, and there was a steady drift home of pupils and masters. In due course I had to follow and we were all back home in time for the real war and the 'Blitz'. These were exciting days for a youngster, with father in the Home Guard, mother an Air Raid Warden, and myself at the ARP Post as messenger boy. Air raids were frequent on Merseyside, resulting in nearly 4,000 killed, over 7000 injured, nearly 11,000 homes destroyed and 180,000 damaged.

I was invited back on holiday to my evacuee home where the family were very kind and treated me as one of their own. One day when picking winberries on a hillside, a stunning aircraft with slender oval tail fins flew down the valley a little above our level. I never forgot it, realising only later that it must have been an early or prototype Lancaster.

In March 1942, still 16, I joined the Merchant Navy as a wartime radio officer. After a week in convoy we proceeded south alone, zig-zagging most of the time as a precaution against U Boats, on route to Cape Town and Alexandria, taking war supplies to the Eighth Army in Egypt, then back to Cape Town for repairs. We then crossed the south Atlantic to Brazil to collect cargo for home from various places including Rio. Re-crossing the Atlantic, from Ascension Island onwards we were 'escorted' by a gun-boat (which had a smaller gun than ours!) to Freetown, Sierra Leone, where we joined a convoy for home. It was now October. After a week out we were heavily attacked by U Boats over four nights, losing most of the ships on our side of the convoy. It was too rough to lower lifeboats. More ships than ever were sunk on the fourth night including a troop ship returning with Italian prisoners of war. Two ships dropped back to pick up survivors but both were torpedoed shortly afterwards. The Commodore's and Vice Commodore's ships had already been sunk. The escort of four corvettes was ineffective and inadequate, due no doubt to the invasion of Tunisia which was about to take place and we were a low priority.

We dreaded another night and there was anxiety when smoke was spotted on the horizon but it turned out to be one of the Yankee four-funnelled destroyers that had been gifted to Britain, which then took over the convoy. In the afternoon a Catalina flying boat arrived and circled the convoy until dusk. I still bless that Catalina. There were no further attacks.

I had decided long before this grim experience that I didn't like life at sea and being only 17 was free to leave as I wished. Watching an aircraft one day in early '43 alerted me to the possibility that I might be able to fly in the air force. I was hooked. Naturally I hoped to be a pilot, but not being in the ATC the Selection Board ruled that out. I thought that I would be offered the role of wireless operator but flight engineers were obviously the current necessity. I had never heard of this role before, thinking it must be some form of maintenance work. They confirmed that it was a full time flying job so I accepted. Later, when I realised that I would be a member of an operational crew, I was delighted.

I commenced life in the RAF in Sept '43, Air Crew Receiving Centre in St John's Wood, PT in Lord's cricket ground, white flashes in our caps, time off in London with new friends - a wonderful start to service life and our morale. Square bashing at ITW, in RAF Unsworth near Sunderland in November, was more sobering. In due course I arrived, as a member of an all NCO crew, at Waterbeach on 7th August '44 travelling with our kit by road in one of the usual small transport vehicles from LFS (Lancaster Finishing School) at Feltwell in Norfolk. As flight engineer I was dismayed to see, from the Ely Road, Lancasters on the dispersal with radial engines! I didn't know such beasts as Lancaster IIs existed. Seven of our earlier operations were flown in Mk IIs, interspersed with Mk Is. Then it was all Mark Is with an occasional Mk III and I must say that I was far happier in these Merlin engined Lancasters, with their ceiling up to 23,000 ft.

Our first operation was a daylight on the marshalling yards at Lens in N France, with the unforgettable first sight of flak bursts ahead. Over the target, a squadron aircraft directly behind was struck in the nose by a bomb from above, which didn't explode. Wally, our rear gunner, saw bits and papers fall away followed by the body of the bomb aimer. Our second operation on the night of 13/ 14th August was to Russelsheim, where flying bomb and aircraft parts were being manufactured at the Opel works. This was our diciest 'op', our two gunners firing simultaneously at two different night fighters, both claimed as 'probables'. In the vicious corkscrew the hatch cover above the pilot's head flew off with a bang, sucking up the navigator's black-out curtain. That we turned the wrong way out of the target area, and over Mainz, was understandable.

A line of Bristol Hercules-powered Lancaster Mk IIs was not what Harry Dison expected when he arrived at RAF Waterbeach. They were subsequently replaced by the Merlin-engined variant, which he much preferred.

After 10 ops Richie was promoted to Flying Officer. By now the rest of us had moved into quarters in the sergeant's mess. Richie would visit by climbing in through one of our windows and on occasion don a jacket and join us in the mess.

I still hoped to re-muster after the tour for pilot training if possible and spent hours on the Link trainer. Richie was good to me, allowing me to take over occasionally. As he had to climb out of his seat for this the rest of the crew were none too happy about it, especially one day when he set off to visit the rear gunner to see what it was like at the tail end. He also took me up for dual control in the station Oxford and over the years we have remained good friends.

Later in life I joined a flying club and finally flew solo when I was 65. I'm sure that it was just as much a thrill then as it would have been in my younger days.

Group Captain Michael Wyatt DFC

RECOLLECTIONS OF 514 SQUADRON

As a Wing Commander I joined 514 Squadron as Commanding Officer at the age of 33 years on 24th May 1944 having entered the RAF in 1934. The Squadron was a good one and easy to command as I had the support of three excellent Flight Commanders. However, shortly after my arrival one of these Flight Commanders completed his tour of operations and he transferred to a second tour of operations with No 7 Pathfinder Squadron. He was replaced by an equally good Squadron Leader who had been a flying instructor just prior to his posting to 514. Also, shortly after my arrival the Squadron began to re-equip with Lancaster Mark III aircraft with Merlin in-line engines as opposed to the radial engined Mark IIs.

During my time with the Squadron I made recommendations for a number of decorations for many brave acts by crews in the air. These were mainly DFCs with a few DSOs. As one example, following a raid on Hamburg, one aircraft had most of the tail plane shot away, but the pilot managed to fly the aircraft home without further incident. Unfortunately, on a later flight this pilot was killed and I can no longer recall his name. He was awarded a DSO.

One of the most impressive raids was the one on D Day which consisted of daylight bombing of the gun site at Ouistreham before the troop landings. As a squadron we supplied 18 aircraft for this raid with no losses.

There were many memorable occasions, one of which was the visit of the American film star Edward G Robinson who spent 24 hours with the squadron trying to get background information on a day in the life of a bomber squadron for a film which was to be made. He found his visit a very moving but enjoyable experience, being particularly moved at the briefing. In fact the film was never made.

Another occasion I remember was the visit of King George VI to hold an investiture in the field when several decorations were made.

I also remember vividly the day a bomb exploded after falling off the bomb rack and blew up the aircraft and damaged several others in the dispersal point. Sadly several ground crew were killed.

On a happier note, on Christmas Day 1944, the Squadron was stood down and I was able to broadcast this over the Tannoy and wish everyone a Happy Christmas.

After the allies had overrun Paris we had a visit by two French young women who had been part of the French Resistance Movement and had helped several British airmen to escape to safety. They were visiting the Squadron to find out what life on a bomber station was really like.

Towards the end of my time with 514 Squadron the aircraft began to be equipped with GH making bombing more precise and the Squadron began to

The Squadron and Flight Commanders of 514 Sqn in October 1943, along with the leaders of crew specialisms. W/Cdr Arthur Samson (front, centre) is flanked by S/Ldr Barney Reid, 'A' Flight (left) and S/Ldr Alan Roberts, 'B' Flight (right).

attack synthetic oil production units which were small. GH was not popular because it involved daylight flying.

I left the Squadron on 7th February 1945 to take up a posting to the Air Ministry in the new Directorate of Navigation as the Assistant Director.

Michael Wyatt

January 1999

The Squadron

514 Squadron was formed on 1st September 1943 within No 3 Group of Bomber Command, initially at Foulsham in Norfolk. It was transferred on 23rd November '43 to Waterbeach, north of Cambridge, where it remained until disbanded on 22nd August '45, shortly after the end of WWII.

The Squadron was initially equipped with Lancaster IIs, powered by four Hercules radial engines. These aircraft were gradually replaced during the summer of '44 by Lancaster Is and IIIs, powered by Merlin in-line engines manufactured by Rolls Royce and Packard respectively.

Although 514 acted often in the role of a main force bomber Squadron, a sufficient number of its aircraft were equipped with GH, a development of the navigational system Gee, which enabled the Squadron to locate precise targets within range of this equipment and even to bomb such targets effectively through cloud when necessary. These attacks were generally carried out in daylight by relatively small numbers of aircraft, and became an increasing role for 514 and the few other GH-equipped squadrons.

The normal complement of aircraft on the Squadron was 30, shared between A, B and C Flights. Only on very rare occasions did the number of aircraft despatched to a target approach the full strength. The average number of Squadron sorties on a target was 17, numbers generally being greater on night attacks and fewer on the smaller and more frequent daylight operations. Long distance targets such as Berlin could only be reached during the long nights of winter or near winter. Fighter cover was a necessity for daylight operations.

As with many other squadrons, aircrews were mainly comprised of men from the United Kingdom, although many crews had one or more members from Australia, Canada or New Zealand and occasionally from elsewhere. Squadron losses amounted to 80 aircraft; 66 missing and 14 crashed.

The Airfields

Foulsham Airfield was situated in Norfolk to the east of Foulsham village and opened in May 1942, joining 2 Group the next month. Still far from ready, it was not until October that Nos 98 and 180 RAF Squadrons arrived with their twin engined (American) Mitchell bombers. The first offensive operation was on 11th January '43 when three out of twelve Mitchells were shot down by FW 190s on a low level daylight attack.

Gun and turret problems retarded further operations until May, the poor state of the muddy airfield and primitive accommodation not helping. Horsa gliders also arrived for storage and No 12 Glider MU was based there for a year. The Mitchells left in August '43.

3 Group took over on 1st September and 514 Squadron started to form, taking two months to reach operational status, the first operational flight being on 3rd November. 1678 Conversion Flight, also equipped with Lancaster IIs, moved to Foulsham on 16th Sept to supply crews to 514. Apart from a handful of 'gardening' (mine laying) operations, the first bombing attack by the Squadron was on 3rd November 1943 when four aircraft took off to join an attack on a target in Dusseldorf.

On 18th November, seven a/c went to Mannheim and two a/c went to Berlin. The first loss to the Squadron was from the Mannheim group, a Lancaster piloted by F/O Thomas. The third bombing attack by the Squadron was on the night of Nov 22nd when four a/c were despatched to Berlin. The final Operation from Foulsham was on the following night, Nov 23rd, when three a/c went to Berlin, but returned to Waterbeach, thus combining the last operation from Foulsham with the move to the Squadron's new base in Cambridgeshire.

Both units moved to Waterbeach on 23rd November 1943.

On 25th November, 192 Squadron arrived at Foulsham, this being a specialist squadron monitoring enemy radio and radar transmissions and later engaged in countermeasures. They flew Halifaxes,

21

The main runway at Waterbeach, from where most operations commenced.

Mosquitoes and Wellingtons and had vacated Feltwell to leave it clear for 3 Group's Lancaster Finishing School. 100 Group (Bomber Support Group) soon acquired both Foulsham and 192 Squadron. By the summer of '44 this Squadron was playing a vital role in the bombing offensive. It was joined later, in '45, by 462 Squadron RAAF. The war over, both Squadrons were disbanded by Sept '45 and the airfield was soon vacated.

Little can now be seen of the old airfield apart from a few hangars and the fire station building. Most of the runways and perimeter track have been returned to farmland, but a section of the northern end of one runway still remains.

Waterbeach Airfield four miles North of Cambridge was initiated when the land was requisitioned in 1939. Hangar construction was well underway by mid-1940 and the aerodrome was festooned with poles and trip wires to prevent an enemy landing. These hazards were cleared away later in the year and then the Germans did come on Feb 3rd 1941, in a Dornier, and dropped a stick of nine bombs along the face of the western hangar and damaged the control tower and runway.

Waterbeach opened on January 11th 1941 having good accommodation up to pre-war standards. With runways almost complete, Wellingtons Ic of 99 Squadron flew in on March 19th 1941. There was still plenty of mud when it rained, as the grass had still to take hold, but dust was the problem in March when the Squadron took off for Cologne. So much of it was thrown up that only six crews could get airborne. The Squadron also started to receive a few Wellington IIs which could carry the 4,000 lb 'Cookie'. The first Berlin raid from Waterbeach took place on April 9th '41. The Squadron stood by to attack the battleship Bismarck on May 25th and the next day searched for the Hipper.

On Dec 8th '41, Q Queenie set off for Aachen but turned back due to engine failure. On final approach the other engine cut. The aircraft crashed, caught fire and then the 4,000 lb Cookie exploded - after the crew had raced to safety. 99 Squadron, with its Wellingtons, left for overseas in March '42. Stirlings began to arrive at Waterbeach in November 1941 for No.1651 Heavy Conversion Unit, formed in Jan '42, and these large aircraft formed the scene for almost two years pending the arrival of 514 Squadron in November '43 accompanied by 1678 Conversion Flight. Waterbeach also became the head of 33 Base, an administrative grouping of three airfields.

The Lancaster II was gradually phased out in favour of Mks I and III, flying their last sorties on 23 Sept '44, resulting in 1678 Conversion Flight being disbanded.

Following the disbanding of 514 Squadron on 27th August 1945 due to the cessation of hostilities, 47 Group, Transport Command, came in mid-September with Liberators of 59 and 220 Squadrons. They quickly started trooping flights to India and the Middle East, but these petered out in the New Year. In August '46, Avro Yorks of 51 Squadron arrived as transports, mainly operating to India. In Nov/Dec '47 they were replaced by Dakotas of 18, 53, 62 and 77 Squadrons of 46 Group. These aircraft would soon be engaged in the Berlin Airlift commencing in the summer of 1948. All of these transport Squadrons, including a late corner, 24 Squadron, were eventually disbanded between Dec '49 and Mar 1950.

Fighter Command took control of Waterbeach in April 1950, with Nos 63 and 56 Squadrons flying Meteors. 56 Squadron received its first Supermarine Swift in Feb '54 but these aircraft proved troublesome and in March '55 the Swifts were withdrawn and replaced with Meteors, which in turn were replaced again with Hunter 5s. 63 Squadron switched to Hunter 6s in Nov '56. Further fighter aircraft changes and Squadron replacements took place until the Hunters of No 54 Squadron finally left for West Raynham in early August 1963.

Sadly, flying at Waterbeach had almost finished, but circuits were flown here by Varsities from 5 FTS Oakington until they were withdrawn, and a few similar flights were made by Oakington's Jetstreams.

The airfield is presently occupied by the Royal Engineers and Burma Star Day celebrations have recently brought aircraft back to the runway.

An Introduction to 514 Squadron

by Eric Basford - Engine Fitter, 'A' Flight.

Some Technical Aspects.

The Lancaster II had Bristol Hercules, air cooled, sleeve valve, radial engines, fitted with Rotol electric (variable pitch) propellers with wooden blades. Their performance was akin to that of the Mk.I and Mk.III Lancasters, with a maximum speed of 265 mph at 14,000ft and a cruising speed of 170 mph. It had a superior rate of climb up to 18,000ft but progress above that level declined somewhat. A few earlier Mk.IIs had Hercules V1 engines but the majority had Hercules XV ls. Very few Lancaster IIs were manufactured, 115 Squadron at Witchford being the only other squadron in 3 Group to have them, In fact there were only four other squadrons in the whole of Bomber Command with Mk IIs. In an accident or crash, the wooden Rotol propeller blades soon broke off. This invariably saved the engine, but meant that very large splinters of wood were flying about at the time.

On the other hand, on the Lancaster ls and Ills, the metal blades of the DH Hydromatic propellers bent backwards when they hit the ground and often bent the propeller shaft on the engine as well. Lancasters I and III. The Squadron had been completely re-equipped by these marks of Lancaster by the end of September '44, all fitted with Merlin in-line engines. On the Mk I, these Rolls Royce engines were British made with SU carburettors. The Mk.III had Packard built Merlins equipped with Stromberg injection carburettors. There was no significant change in performance between the two marks, nor any difference in their external features.

All Lancasters received after about November '44, had propeller blades with parallel edges and rounded tips, loosely described as paddle blades.

Identification markings.
The Squadron identification letters were JI for A and B Flight aircraft, but A2 for those in C Flight. The Squadron establishment was 30 aircraft, 10 in each flight, so this method overcame the shortage of identity letters for individual aircraft. C Flight used letters A to L again, these aircraft being loosely referred to as A2, E2 etc. All identification letters were painted in brick red on each side of the fuselage. Until early 1943, identification letters had always been in white, and the redesigned roundels on the fuselage were also introduced at this time.

With the increase of daylight operations in Aug '44 and to assist identification for formation flying, the propeller spinners of A Flight were painted red, spinners of B Flight were painted yellow and those of C Flight were blue. About this time Squadron aircraft equipped With the GH bombing device had two yellow bands painted horizontally across the top half of each tail fin. Normally two aircraft without this equipment would formate on one of these distinctively marked aircraft, triggering the release of their own bombs the instant their bomb aimers saw the first bomb dropping from the GH aircraft.

Bomb 'Hang Ups'.
Occasionally, it happened that the crew of an aircraft having bombed the target would find that they had a 'hang up', i.e. a bomb still in position on its rack. Attempts would then be made to shake it clear on the way home. Sometimes they were successful, sometimes not. However, the vibrations on landing often dislodged the bomb and the aircraft would taxi round to its dispersal with the bomb resting on the bomb doors. In such circumstances, the pilot would not open the bomb doors before shutting off the engines, as was the normal practice with Lancasters. The aircrew invariably left the aircraft smartly and the bomb could usually be discerned through the joint of the two bomb doors. The armourers would be called to deal at once with the potential hazard. They would arrive with a bomb trolley, one of their hand Winches and several old bedding biscuits (small mattresses). After positioning the biscuits under the bomb doors, one would go into the cockpit and everyone else would stand well clear. As the man in the cockpit put the bomb door lever to 'open', the

bomb would slowly emerge and suddenly fall onto the soft bedding underneath. The other armourers would then return to the aircraft and winch up the bomb, lower it onto the trolley and tow it back to the bomb dump. The whole procedure was simple, if crude, but it never failed as far as I know.

Delayed Action Hang Ups. Dealing with a hang-up could be more complicated if the bomb happened to be a delayed action type. In that event, the armourers would examine the bomb for signs of staining, which would indicate that the acid bottle had broken and the bomb was set to explode, after a time interval. If the bottle had broken, the bomb was winched back onto its rack in the bomb bay. One of the senior pilots, often a Flight Commander, would take-off with it as soon as possible accompanied by only one other senior aircrew member. They would fly out to a designated area in The Wash to dump the problem bomb. That routine never failed either as far as I am aware.

On Station Entertainment.

In the early years of the war 'the flicks' were the main form of off-duty entertainment on RAF stations. Training stations had purpose built cinemas that were open every evening and, apart from being smaller, were comparable with those in small towns. Admission charges were low, programmes up-to-date, and projection and presentation of a professional standard. Cinemas on operational stations were no match for those on training stations. The cinema at RAF Waterbeach, although located in a room over the airmen's mess, was open every evening, had up-to-date films changed regularly, and was well patronised. We also had the advantage of several excellent modern cinemas in Cambridge.

From the spring of 1944 onwards we also had some top quality live entertainment on the station. These ENSA shows were put on in the NAAFI, where there was a good permanent stage at one end. It meant that the NAAFI would have to be closed for that evening. I recall that we had Stanford Robinson with the BBC orchestra. James Mason (the most recent film and stage star of the day) acted in a play at Waterbeach. Then we had a few variety shows in which some stars of the London stage appeared. Pat Kirkwood,

Entertainment was never in short supply at RAF Waterbeach. This photograph is from a New Year's Eve dance, believed to be in 1944.

glamorous vocalist, is one name that springs to mind. All in all, we enjoyed some excellent professional live entertainment at Waterbeach in 1944.

Perhaps as a consequence of these top showbiz people, an amateur concert party and an amateur dramatic society were formed from airmen and Waafs serving at Waterbeach in 1944. The concert party staged some excellent shows for us but I do not remember any production from the dramatic society. General movements, i.e. postings to and from the station, always created major problems for such activities, since the loss of just one key performer could be disastrous.

Small Beginnings

Corporal E Melluish, 'Mel', an armourer, tells us that our Squadron had an inauspicious start:

I was the very first person to be allocated to 514 Squadron having returned from three and a half years in Iraq in August 1943. I was posted to RAF Foulsham where on arrival was informed that there must be a mistake as there was no such Squadron. The orderly room made enquiries but told me to report to the station armoury pending further enquiries. The armoury had a corporal and another ranker. The corporal was junior to me and I believe saw me as an intruder into his domain. He didn't know what to do about me so I solved his problem by going back home on a further 7 days leave. On my return I found that several other bods had arrived and a new squadron was forming.

Cpl 'Mel'Melluish found that no one expected him when he arrived at RAF Foulsham, the first member of 514 Sqn to do so. As an armourer he was to be kept very busy over the following two years. This photo shows Lancaster Mk.II LL678, A2-L performing an engine test with a 4,000lb 'Cookie' in front of her on a trailer.

Leslie Weddle, Flight Engineer

The crew of Lancaster II 'C' Charlie, LL727, 'C' Flight.

Pilot F / O Louis Greenburgh
Navigator Sgt Pat Butler
B / Aimer F/ Sgt Don Bament
W/Op A/G Sgt Gordon Stromberg
F /E Sgt Leslie Weddle
M / U Gunner F / Sgt Fred Carey
R / Gunner Sgt Colin Drake

Some crews had more than their fair share of troubles. Leslie, then aged 19 relates:

After spending October and November 1943 flying Stirlings on 620 Squadron Chedburgh, Bury St Edmunds, we returned to 1678 Conversion Unit, Waterbeach, converting to Lancaster IIs and joined 514 Squadron in December 1943.

Our first operation from Waterbeach was on 29th December 1943. Flying in spare aircraft 'S' Sugar we took off for Berlin. Following one or two fighter attacks we finally reached our target, released our bombs and headed for home. After leaving the target we were twice attacked by JU.88s puncturing at least one of our petrol tanks. After a while I informed the Skipper we were losing quite a lot of petrol and we may not reach England and would probably have to ditch. We flew on as long as possible but as the engines started cutting out the Skipper ordered us to ditching stations. After a successful ditching we eventually got out but had to inflate the dinghy as it was only partly inflated.

We ditched about 10pm, 70 miles east of Yarmouth. We spent an horrendous night - high winds and waves and by daylight we felt pretty desperate – seven

Lou Greenburgh's Lancaster DS821, JI-S, still afloat in the North Sea the day after ditching.

The Greenburgh crew were rescued after sixteen hours adrift in the North Sea.

A true leader. Wing Commander Arthur Samson DFC takes a well-earned break at home. 514 Sqn's first CO, he endeared himself to his crews by personally flying a Lancaster over the North Sea in an attempt to find the Greenburgh crew. This mission was successful, ensuring that the crew of seven was saved.

very wet bedraggled airmen in a partly inflated dinghy. We were eventually spotted by Wing Commander Sampson of 514 Sqn, who, at daybreak, scrambled a scratch crew as he knew time was very valuable, and one of his crews was somewhere in the North Sea. Shortly after, a Liberator arrived and dropped a spare dinghy which was greatly appreciated as we were rather low in the sea. A high speed launch was then directed to our position and we got picked up about 2pm. Needless to say we were very relieved after spending 16 hours in the North Sea. We spent the night in hospital and after a checkup Wing Commander Sampson flew down to Coltishall and gave us a lift back to Waterbeach. We were then given 16 days leave - one day for every hour spent in the drink. All this entitled us to become members of the 'Goldfish Club' of which I am still a member.

A few more Ops - Stuttgart - Le Mans - Berlin - Frankfurt - Frankfurt, and finally Berlin on 24th March 1944, where, after a rough trip there, the Skipper ordered us to bale out. The bomb aimer left first, followed by myself. The navigator was to follow me, but the 'plane veered violently and he lost his parachute out of the escape hatch. Also the rear gunner was trapped in his turret. So while the two of us were drifting down to earth the skipper decided to try and get the 'plane back to England - which he did, and was awarded the bar to his D.F.C. - won when we ditched. All this I found out when I was released as a P.O.W. Baling out and saving my life by parachute enabled me to become a member of the 'Caterpillar Club'.

I found life on the Squadron very pleasant and satisfying with the occasional exciting episode, like the time we took off on air test only to find the pitot head tube cover still in place. After a few anxious minutes a second aircraft from 514 was flying alongside to give us an indication of our speed and guided us in to a perfect landing.

The highlight of my life was at the 1993 Squadron Reunion where I met Pat Butler (Navigator) and Fred Carey (Mid Upper Gunner). What a re-union after 50 years.

Louis Greenburgh, Pilot

Louis Greenburgh with original crew. Back row (left to right): Gordon Stromberg, W/Op; Leslie Weddle, F/E; Fred Carey, M/U/G; Pat Butler, Nav. Front row: Colin Drake, R/G; Lou Greenburgh, Pilot; Don Bament, B/A.

It has been the author's good fortune to have a sister in Canada who (apart from locating a Canadian fellow crew member) has been able to trace and put him in verbal contact with Louis Greenburgh, This led to the receipt of a book entitled "DFC & BAR", written by Lou's son, Edwin Greenburgh, covering all the dramatic facets of his father's life, and from which the following account has been extracted. It has also been rewarding for the author to have been of assistance in putting Lou back in touch with some of his old crew members.

Louis Greenburgh, DFC & Bar, was 514 Squadron's most memorable pilot. He was born in 1916 in Winnipeg, Manitoba, of Jewish parents; his father a Russian immigrant and his mother, a refugee he believes, from Poland.

His parents separated three months later in Toronto, then an uncle accompanied him and his mother back to the west. For two years they scraped a living in various places before settling in the small northern town of Rosthem in Saskatchewan. Unwanted and unloved, his mother married again when he was six and from then on he was regularly beaten. Eventually they arrived back in Winnipeg when Lou was aged about 11.

His accomplishments at school were minimal, a deprived home life and bouts of truancy not helping. One day he went with a friend beyond the city limits to an airstrip named Stevenson Field and watched airplanes take off and land. He was fascinated and spent much of his spare time there. He read all he could about flying and the Great War aces who became his heroes, and he dreamed of being a pilot.

He left home for good when just 17, riding the freight trains to the west with two friends, finding occasional work where they could. This was the time of the Great Depression in 1933, their companions often hoboes and other down and outs. There was always the danger of slipping under the wheels of a moving train when boarding, or losing hold when clinging to the icy roof of a swaying box car. He rode the rails for three years experiencing a variety of jobs and work camps and got to know almost every soup kitchen in western Canada.

During this period he tried to join the Royal Canadian Air Force, hoping that he might become an aircraft mechanic, but there was little chance with his lack of credentials and his application came to nothing.

Eventually he fell in with an activist group for political and economic reform, and joined in the march to Ottawa. This led to the Regina Riot where Lou was arrested along with others, spending two months in jail before charges were dropped. While there an Irish guard befriended him and after hearing that Lou was interested in flying, advised him to go by cattle boat to England and try to join the RAF. So at the age of 21 he came to England in 1937, some two years before the outbreak of war. His persistence to join the RAF finally paid off and he was offered the lowly role of ACII General Duties, commencing service life in July 1937 for little pay, but content with three square meals a day and the hope that if he worked hard he might one day make flight mechanic.

His first flight came when he was taken up in the open cockpit of a Hawker Hind. He volunteered to be an air gunner so that he could fly again. In 1938 this was just a temporary duty in addition to his usual chores. He was given a badge, the winged bullet, and became an instant gunner. Eventually he did become a flight mechanic, training at Manston and St Athan in South Wales (where later, Flight Engineers would receive their ground schooling). Lou's hard work paid off and he came top of his class, completing the course in July 1939.

One night in 1940, at Bassingbourne, Cambridgeshire, he awoke to what he thought was the sound of an enemy bomber. It went away but returned, then their barrack room was hit by a bomb. Lou was tossed into the air, then jumped through a broken window into a bomb crater where he sheltered with others. The airman in the next bed to him and his friend in the opposite barracks were killed.

Early in 1941 he heard that a selection board for Pilots was at the base. With little hope he applied. The written maths questions were beyond his level, but he protested, stating that hard work and enthusiasm would make up for what he lacked in education. Against all the odds he was accepted.

Lou crossed the Atlantic, by freighter in convoy in February '42 to Canada, on route to Ponca City, Oklahoma for flying training with the U.S. Army Air Corps. They flew in Stearman biplanes, which he loved. He worried a lot as many were being washed out, but his first solo was one of the greatest moments of his life. His first night solo was different. Barely into the circuit he was hit by a heavy rain squall and couldn't see the ground or anything else. The Stearman had the minimum of instruments and he couldn't tell up from down. Finally, after getting into a spin he somehow levelled out, the wheels struck the ground hard and the aircraft pitched over in a forward roll, leaving him hanging upside down by his harness. In spite of his fears, he wasn't washed out and completed his pilot's course in September '42, becoming commissioned soon afterwards with the rank of Pilot Officer.

He returned to England for twin engine training on Airspeed Oxfords, and then proceeded to O.T.U. to crew-up and train on Wellingtons. On Sept 2nd 1943 they were posted to 1651 H.C.U. at Waterbeach, where they acquired a flight engineer and flew the massive four-engined Stirling. At this time, 514 Squadron was just starting to form at Foulsham. Lou's crew members were:

Navigator - Sgt Pat Butler B/Aimer - F/Sgt Don Bament W/Op -Sgt Gordon Stromberg ('Strommy'), F/Eng - Sgt Leslie Weddle ('Geordie') M.U.Gunner - F/ Sgt Fred Carey R. Gunner - Sgt Colin Drake ('Connie').

Posting to 620 Squadron at Chedburgh followed, where Lou had his first operational experience as 2nd Dicky in a Stirling with another crew, in a night attack on Kassel. The gunners claimed hits on an attacking FW190, losses that night being 24. Lou and his crew took part in Air Sea Rescue flights and mine laying operations with this Squadron and one night they had to get down quickly, landing at a small satellite airfield with only a grass landing field. Lou, unable to see a thing, received taxiing directions from the controller who had them on his screen. Moving forward as instructed, a falling sensation accompanied by a loud splash announced they had 'ditched' the Stirling in a flooded gravel pit, with only the upper parts of the aircraft remaining above water. Fortunately they were not blamed for this mishap.

Lou and his crew joined 1678 Conversion Flight at Waterbeach in December 1943 for conversion to Lancaster IIs, and then joined 514 Squadron which had also moved to Waterbeach. Their first operation was on the night of 29th December. They expected it to be an easy one, but the target was Berlin. The long distance to the target and the severity of its defences could deter the bravest of crews. 457 Lancasters, 252 Halifaxes and 3 Mosquitoes took part. Spoof targets were Dusseldorf Leipzig and Magdeburg.

At dusk they entered S Sugar's dark fuselage and took up their positions. Lou, now a Flying Officer, carried out his many checks, as did each crew member. Taxiing in the fading twilight he could see the outline of the row of bombers. In turn, the green light signalled they were clear for take-off and Lou opened the throttles, progressively at first to counter the initial swing, and then to full power as the aircraft gathered speed. At 10,000 feet he ordered the crew to don oxygen masks. Hundreds of bombers were all around, but in the darkness none were visible. In the distance he saw odd bursts from the German flak ships in the North Sea but paid them little attention. Their course was first set to the Friesian Islands.

About an hour later the mid-upper reported a twin engined aircraft astern, but the gunners disagreed as to its identity. Lou started to take mild evasive action when there was an explosion in the starboard wing. 'Geordie' (Les Weddle, flight engineer) soon reported loss of fuel from the starboard outer tank. Lou considered turning back but thought they might be easy prey for fighters. Berlin wasn't too distant now and he could see the city's searchlights ahead. The sight of the approaching target area was awesome, combining searchlights, flak, fighter flares, explosions and burning aircraft. The wings of their aircraft seemed to stretch across the whole city. Last minute directions came from the Master Bomber. Cloud was obscuring the target and they were directed to make their target run on sky-marker target indicators ('Wanganui'). The pilot needed to maintain a constant heading and altitude for this method to have any chance of accuracy, which also increased the likelihood of being hit by bombs from aircraft above.

They bombed at last and turned westwards for home, Lou finding the aircraft increasingly difficult to control. They ran into storm conditions with bad turbulence and icing and he tried to climb above it, using more precious fuel. Geordie protested, doubting if they had enough fuel to reach the coast but they all decided to stay with the aircraft rather than bale out over enemy territory. Slowly they gained altitude and were over the North Sea before the storm cleared and the turbulence ceased. Tracer ripped past and Lou hauled hard to starboard as a FW 190 flashed by. Round and round they corkscrewed with this tenacious fighter until they finally lost him.

Fuel shortage was now critical and Connie, the rear gunner, was yelling, "An airplane with a beard. It's an airplane with a beard. A Fortress with a beard! It's coming after us." As the engines cut successively, Lou instructed the wireless operator, Strommy, to start the MAY DAY routine and get a fix and then ordered the crew into their forward crash positions. The last engine cut and the descent was difficult with control almost lost at one stage. Lou opened his side window, dividing his attention between the open window, the altimeter and the airspeed indicator, almost frantic for some clue as to when to pull the nose up. He could see nothing and accepted the fact that he was about to die. With the altimeter at zero, salt water burst through the open window as he hauled back hard on the wheel. They skipped and bounced on wave tops, then the tail section broke off and the canopy shattered as they rammed into a wall of water. He woke up coughing, up to his chin in ice-cold water. Miraculously the cockpit began to rise and most of the water drained out. Hands unclipped his harness and Geordie and Strommy dragged him out of the upper escape hatch. He lost his balance falling into the sea taking Geordie with him, but somehow they made it to the half inflated, open life raft and were helped aboard. Water sloshed back and forth, and baling was impossible.

Sleet pelted his face and stung his eyes, but he saw that everyone had made it to the life raft. The aircraft still floating and rolling around in the waves was a danger to them, but fortunately the cord attaching them to the aircraft broke and they drifted downwind, but were still in peril from the massive waves. Water cascaded aboard and Strommy was washed over the side, but luckily kept a grip on the safety line around the raft and they were able to pull him back in. The night was sheer hell. They tried to keep each other's spirits up but could only keep it going for so long, and by morning could barely move and had pretty well given up hope. The dinghy had been leaking all night but they found the pump and for the next two hours took turns pumping more air into the deflated sections. It was bitterly cold in the North Sea in late December, and it was only their flying suits, acting in the manner of divers' wet suits, that kept them alive.

Only Connie stayed active, pointing to imaginary ships and planes insisting they had been chased by a bearded Fortress. Even without beards, they all knew that American Fortresses in Europe only flew on daylight operations! At about 0915 hrs Connie pointed to the horizon and yelled, "It's a Lanc, it's a Lanc", then Lou saw it and fired off a flare. The Lancaster, flown by the C.O. Wing Commander Sampson out searching for them, turned and began to circle. Later, supplies were dropped, but were swept away. At about 1230 the rescue launch arrived, though boarding was difficult in the heavy seas. Lou, too weak to move, was lifted aboard. Prior to going on leave, Lou, concerned about Connie's 'hallucinations', ensured that he would be dropped from his crew. On returning, Lou was awarded the D.F.C., then sent on a short lecture tour instructing other pilots in the art of ditching a Lancaster II. Then it was back to operations.

Their thirteenth operation, on the night of 24 March '44, was also their fourth to Berlin. The north wind, far stronger than forecast, was of such strength that many navigators couldn't believe their own figures, resulting in the bomber force being well scattered. Well south of their intended course across Denmark, they became coned by searchlights, providing a brilliant target for fighters. Every evasive trick Lou tried seemed hopeless until he went into a powered dive, narrowly missing another Lancaster, which itself became the coned aircraft. They regained height to 21,000 feet by the time they reached Berlin, but the Pathfinders had not yet marked the target. The rear gunner shouted for corkscrew action and tracer flashed by. They saw a bomber in flames, then a second and a third. Lou wanted to drop the bombs and go, this was no place to be hanging around, but at last the Master Bomber spoke and they saw the target indicators and started their bombing run. As they bombed, the canopy shattered under a hail of fire from a fighter and the starboard wing burst into flame. Not realising he had lost both starboard engines, Lou opened the throttles, the port wing came up and they rolled over. Completely out of control they accelerated into a spiral dive and as smoke filled the cockpit Lou gave the order to bale out. Fred Carey left his turret and jumped. Geordie or Don opened the forward escape hatch and they both dived through. Pat, the navigator, fumbled with his clip-on parachute as he made his way to the same escape hatch. The tail gunner called to say he couldn't get out, then managed to free himself and jumped. The aircraft was going round and round in a circle as Lou tried to regain control but it seemed that in no time they had fallen to 7,000 feet. Lou crawled down to the nose followed by Strommy, to find Pat still in the cramped area. The din was incredible, all three shouting and the wind roaring through the open hatch. Pat wouldn't jump. "I can't," he yelled, "I've lost my parachute."

Lou, unable to abandon his navigator, struggled back against the centrifugal force of the rotating bomber and somehow regained his seat. Instinctively he shut the power, and with the imbalance corrected the plane started to respond. He pulled out of the dive at under 2,000feet, then gave it some throttle, only then realising that he had two dead engines on the starboard side. Pat joined him in the cockpit and Strommy, who had decided to stay aboard, got busy putting fires out with an extinguisher. The navigation equipment was ruined and Lou wondered how any of them had survived the hail of metal that had perforated the cockpit.

They flew west at a height of about 5,000 feet, all they could manage, and with both starboard engines dead the aircraft flew crabwise and uneconomically, so they were concerned about fuel. The starboard wing continued to burn. Near Walcheren, they came under fire from coastal batteries and flak ships. The continued strain on Lou's arms and legs was becoming almost unbearable but they still opted for Waterbeach rather than Woodbridge. Practically out of fuel they landed heavily on the grass alongside the runway, causing further damage to the long suffering Lancaster.

Pat now left the crew and as four members were POWs in Germany only faithful Strommy remained. Five new members therefore joined the crew:

Navigator - F/ Sgt Ronald Fox; B/Aimer - F/Sgt Eric Rippingale; F/Eng - Sgt Collingwood; M.U.G. - F/Sgt F Casey; R.G. - Sgt R Woosham

On 7th June'1944 (D DAY plus One) they were briefed for a night attack on one of three railway targets in the French town of Massy-Palaiseau (south of Paris) with the object of preventing German reinforcements getting to the Normandy battle front. 75 Aircraft took part in these attacks. Lou had a 'second dicky' with him on this trip, W/O L Sutton, and Lou told him it was a target just across the Channel with nothing to worry about. No one could then know, but losses on this target would be a staggering 17.3%.

They approached the target at 10,000 feet. There was flak all over the place and they could see fighters silhouetted. Lou circled the target once and picked out the markers. Aircraft were going down right and left, the air full of tracer and flak. They made the bombing rim and almost on the point of release the gunners called the pilot to corkscrew. The bombs dropped an instant later and Lou began a violent corkscrew, but by then it was too late. Tracer zoomed past his head and he heard strikes on the fuselage. Fire erupted in the starboard wing behind the inner engine and spread rapidly. He steepened the dive trying to blow out the fire and avoid the tracer but was hit in the starboard outer, which cut. Lou ordered the crew to jump and the bomb aimer and second dicky baled out followed by the engineer and navigator, then the fire seemed to die down and Lou called the remaining crew to hold on. A searchlight caught them and Lou dived to escape only to be coned again, then they were hit by light flak losing rudder control. The rear gunner reported a JU 88 following and they were hit again by cannon shells. Strommy reported he was going and baled out and Lou ordered the gunners to follow.

Lou held on a while, but finally accepting that he would soon be burned alive, dived through the escape hatch into the darkness. Briefly, when his chute opened Lou lost his flying boots and his escape kit slipped out of his tunic, resulting in the loss of his knife, rations, maps, compass and pistol. He landed in an area north of Paris, receiving help from many brave French people, but had some narrow escapes at check points. At one point, he was arrested, but the Prefecture of Police was instrumental in enabling him to regain his freedom. Lou was haunted by the fact that his RAF identity discs were stamped with the word JEW, feeling doomed with or without them. If one house he escaped through a back window when the Germans were entering through the front door to make a search. On another occasion he was pressed into service at the railway station in Trappes, issued with an armband and put into a supervised working party clearing rubble. Fearing his identity would be discovered he had to run the risk of making his escape. One of his most detested experiences was having to spend a few days in what was virtually a freshly dug hole in the ground. Eventually he was taken to an encampment in the Forest of Fretval, where many other RAF and US aircrew were in hiding, and so successfully evaded capture until relieved by advancing US Army units on 11th August 1944.

Lou has always felt guilt stricken over Strommy who had told him, prior to the Massy-Palaiseau operation, that he had met a girl he wished to marry and would stop flying, but Lou persuaded him to do this one last trip. Lou had the brief impression that Strommy was wounded, as he saw him make his way to the escape hatch.

Strommy died on 9th June '44, aged 19. Lou received a Bar to his D.F.C at an investiture in Buckingham Palace on 11th December '45. During his operational flying with 514 Squadron Lou suffered and survived 14 attacks by fighters.

Postscript. Years later when flying on the Berlin Airlift, Lou met up with a pilot, Taff Richardson, with whom he had trained during the war. He astounded Lou by telling him that he had witnessed Lou's aircraft going down on the night it ditched. Returning home over the North Sea they had seen what appeared to be a radial- engined Lancaster in trouble, so had followed it down for some distance and reported its position. Taff had been flying a 'Radar Fortress', a hush-hush electronic countermeasures aircraft used to jam the German radar. He added that his Fortress had a large radar dome called a 'chin dome' under the nose that looked like a beard!

Harry G Darby, Air Bomber

F/O Harry Darby, aged 21, was a bomb aimer with one of the earlier crews to arrive on the Squadron, that of F/S Don Crombie RAAF. Their first trip was to Berlin on 16th December 1943 followed by an attack on Frankfurt on 20th December. On 14th Jan '44 the target was Brunswick and on the way back there was an oxygen failure in the mid-upper gun turret. The gunner, presumably after removing his gloves in trying to rectify the fault, passed out through lack of oxygen. Before his plight was realised he had suffered severe frost bite to his fingers. As a result he was grounded and the crew needed a replacement mid-upper gunner and so Flt Sgt Claude Payne joined the crew from the 'spare bods pool'.

The other crew members were:

Pilot Flt Sgt D C Crombie late twenties (Australian)
Nav Sgt A McPhee " "
W/ Op Sgt M J Tyler aged 20
R/G Sgt H R Hill aged 20
F/ E Sgt B P le Neve Foster aged 21

Harry Darby was contacted in 1990 by the sister and niece of Claude Payne, who was killed in action, as they wished to know about his Squadron life and especially his eventual fate. The following is extracted from the account that Harry then wrote for them.

Claude struck me as being a man of some maturity; after all he was married and was surely in his late twenties at least! He was quietly spoken, had a nice sense of humour and enjoyed a pint or two but never drank to excess. He was good company at crew get-togethers and devoted to his wife Muriel.

Claude's first operation with us was against Berlin on 20 /21st January 1944. Fairly uneventful for us although 35 aircraft were lost. The next night we took off to attack Magdeburg. On approaching the German coast we had an oxygen failure, in the rear turret this time, and Roy Hill passed out. Crombie sensibly decided to turn back. We felt we had been lucky - it was a disastrous raid, 57 bombers being lost including four from our Squadron. This started the legend of Claude's 'scrub rug'.

Claude had a large, shaggy blanket of some sort, which he draped round his legs when flying to keep out the bitter cold. He called it his 'scrub rug' and reckoned if he 'had a word with it' there was a good chance that the operation would be scrubbed, that is to say cancelled or abandoned for one reason or another. Needless to say, any reference to the 'scrub rug' was always made with a twinkle in his eye.

We then participated in the following operations, prior to Nuremberg.

27/28 January	Berlin	33 aircraft lost
30/31 January	Berlin	33 aircraft lost
15/16 February	Berlin	43 aircraft lost
19/20 February	Leipzig	78 aircraft lost
1/2 March	Stuttgart	4 aircraft lost
22/23 March	Frankfurt	33 aircraft lost
26/27 March	Essen	9 aircraft lost

On the night of 15/16 February, I think, returning from Berlin, the bomber stream became rather spread out and we strayed over a heavily defended area between Munster and Osnabruck. We were suddenly coned by about a dozen searchlights which created an enormous blob of light from which it was almost impossible to escape, and shells were soon bursting all around us. I could hear the clatter of shell splinters striking us and feared for the safety of my mates. Crombie worked a miracle by putting the aircraft into a terrific dive and we dropped from 20,000 to 14,000 feet in a matter of seconds, enabling us to escape and race for the Dutch coast and comparative safety.

The Leipzig operation was a shambles - just about everything went wrong for the bombers and right for the German defences. As a result we lost 78 aircraft including four from our Squadron; the second worst night Bomber Command ever had. Our morale distinctly sagged with the realisation that we couldn't expect to go on beating odds like those.

Next came a brief interlude. At the end of February, Crombie was commissioned Pilot Officer and the whole crew was granted special leave to accompany him to London. He had to go to Australia House for certain formalities and to be kitted out. We solemnly formed up and saluted him when he emerged. He said "Thanks mates, now let's find a pub".

Frankfurt on 22/23 March was one of the few occasions when I had a clear view of the ground in the target area and I made a long steady bombing run to be sure of getting our load into the middle of it. Anti-aircraft fire was thick and a shell burst just ahead of us as we were leaving the target. A shell splinter smashed through a front perspex window up on the main flight deck and hit Ben, the Flight Engineer, in the back of the head, killing him instantly. Crombie ordered me up to see if I could succour him in any way, but as I checked that his oxygen mask was working I could feel that the back of his skull was shattered. I became drenched in his blood and took over his duties. We were a very shaken crew when we got back to base. The sands appeared to be running out for us and our morale took another hard knock.

We all slept the following day. Being in a state of mild shock I was put into sick quarters and given a knockout pill. The next day we slow marched behind Ben's coffin to the main gate, then transport to Cambridge railway station and on to Sevenoaks for the funeral. At Ben's home we met his mother and other relations. He was buried at Greatness Cemetery - the six of us flanking the grave and saluting as the coffin was lowered. Claude and the W/Op, both Londoners, went to their homes for the night and we other four went into London and got rather drunk - it seemed to be about the only thing to do.

We were soon in action again, going to Essen on 26th March, Ben's place being taken by Flt Lt Hall, a squadron staff officer. Then came Nuremburg on 30th March. On that morning a replacement F / E, Sgt Jim McGahey a quiet Devonian from Exeter, joined our crew, but we never had a chance to get to know him socially. We came away from final briefing and Wriggled into our flying clothes. Claude looked quite haggard and said that he didn't like the look of this one. I remember saying "Cheer up mate, it may not be too bad, and it will be one nearer the finishing line". He smiled wistfully and said "Perhaps I should have a word with the scrub-rug". The so called Long Leg from the German Frontier near Aachen to the final turning point was a nightmare. The German fighters got into the bomber stream at an early stage in perfect visibility and shot the bombers down like flies. It was possible to see three or four aircraft spinning down in flames at any one time. It was all a truly terrifying experience.

When we turned onto the final leg to the target, the night became much darker and things became a good deal quieter. However I was making preparations for the attack when I spotted a twin-engined aircraft on the port beam flying a parallel course and falling astern of us. I at once alerted the pilot and the gunners and got on with my work. Claude, with the all-round vision afforded by his turret, immediately picked up the German fighter, almost certainly a Junkers 88, and Roy did so soon afterwards, and together they gave a running commentary to prepare Crombie for possible evasive action. Roy reported that the fighter had his navigation lights on and was just out of range. Crombie said "Give the bastard a burst. Let him see we're awake". I heard the rattle of our machine guns, and Roy reported that the fighter had put his lights out. For the next half minute or so there was no activity of any kind. In fact I was just thinking that the fighter had sheared off when suddenly there were three loud bangs on the starboard side. I looked out and saw that the starboard inner engine was on fire. Crombie saw it at the same time, ordered the Flight Engineer to shut the engine down and operate the fire extinguisher located in the engine nacelle. But it was too late as the fire had already spread to the wing in which fuel tanks were located. Crombie obviously realised that the aircraft was doomed and ordered "Bale out, bale out".

On receiving Crombie's order I at once prepared to jump. Roy Hill called on the intercom to say that he couldn't get out of his turret. I felt in a dilemma - whether to open the forward escape hatch and get out as it was my duty to do so thereby clearing the way for three others to follow or to go back to help Roy. I called Crombie to ask if we should go or stay. In a voice of desperation he replied "For Christ's sake get out as quick as you can". I opened the escape hatch and rolled forward into 22,000 feet of very cold dark sky. The Lanc roared over me and I just had a glimpse of the fire in the starboard wing. The time was just after 1.00 am. Andy McPhee still speaks of his relief at getting down into my compartment and finding it empty with the escape hatch open. There can be little doubt that our aircraft went out of control soon afterwards and that the other five lads just couldn't make their escape.

The Lancaster, burning fiercely, crashed with full bomb load just outside the Bavarian village of Eichenhausen, district of Bad Neustadt. No recognisable human remains were found. In 1984 the local German parishioners erected a stone memorial with a bronze cross and plaque bearing the names of the five men who died.

Many years later Harry Darby became convinced that they were the victims of a night fighter equipped with '*Schräge Musik*', a system of upward firing guns. Bomber Command was generally ignorant of this technique in 1944, so it was deadly. He refutes early records that they were attacked by two fighters, based on interrogation of McPhee and himself when they were repatriated. He believes that the Junkers 88 simply lost a little height and slipped underneath them out of their line of vision and calmly fired three cannon shells into their starboard inner engine - the classic form of attack. He also reminds us that the Nuremberg Raid was Bomber Command's greatest disaster. 96 aircraft were missing and many others too damaged to fly again. 545 aircrew were killed and a further 200 wounded or taken prisoner. These casualties were greater than those suffered by Fighter Command in the entire Battle of Britain.

Harry Darby sent his observations to Martin Middlebrook and is quoted in two of his books 'The Berlin Raids' and 'The Nuremberg Raid'. The following notes are extracted from material that Harry had sent in connection with the attacks on Berlin.

We were not equipped with H2S and had no target marking responsibilities. Target location and bomb aiming were made very difficult by the fact that on most, if not all, of my trips to Berlin, the outward route and target area were obscured by thick cloud cover. I have no clear recollection of seeing the ground, or pathfinder ground markers, when over Berlin. Generally I aimed at sky markers put down by pathfinders. Sometimes these would have fallen into the cloud tops by the time we arrived, and the best one could do was to aim at the centre of a general glow coming up from what one could only assume was the target area.

The majority of the operations in which I took part seemed to be beset by foul weather of one sort or another. The clatter of ice particles against the fuselage as they were flung off the tips of the propellers was a nerve shaking experience. Above all we had to contend with thick cloud. My general recollection is that by the time we crossed the enemy coast and certainly by the time we were beyond the range of Gee, we were entirely dependent on dead reckoning navigation, backed up by 'broadcast' winds which sometimes seemed suspect.

Morale remained remarkably high for a number of reasons. Crews went missing of course, but this was an 'accident' that always happened to somebody else. In any case we hardly ever got to know the outcome of losing a crew, and one thought that they had all safely baled out anyway. Replacement crews, keen to get in the fight, were always arriving, and life just went on. The morale of our crew started on a high note. We had been declared ready for operations in November 1943. It was usual for new crews to be 'blooded' on a reasonably short or intermediate range target, however at that time there just weren't any such operations being mounted. It was Berlin over and over again, interspersed only occasionally by some other target involving deep penetration into Germany. On 16th December, presumably because of casualties and pressure for maximum effort, the C.O. sent for Crombie and asked him if we would be prepared to take our chance on Berlin that night. A brief crew conference ensued and we agreed to a man; and what a baptism of fire it turned out to be. We were engaged by a fighter and had an engine knocked out over the target. We struggled back to Waterbeach to find that most of East Anglia lay under dense fog. We were diverted to Downham Market, one of a handful of stations equipped with Fido (fog intense dispersal of). On arrival Crombie called up the control tower and was told "You are turn thirty-six; circle the (radio) beacon at 18,000 feet". This meant that thirty-five other aircraft, stacked at intervals of 500 feet were waiting to land before us. Hoping for some degree of priority, Crombie informed control that we had only three engines, but that cut no ice. After what seemed an eternity, our turn came round and we made our approach. The total gloom gave way to a diffused glow ahead and then suddenly I could see the Fido flares along both sides of the runway. I realised at once that we were too high on our approach and informed the pilot, but he yelled back "I'm buggered if I'm going to overshoot (go round again) on a night like this". He just dropped the old kite onto the runway with an awful bump. We ran off the end into what looked like a cabbage field, but miraculously Crombie swung her round onto the perimeter track and we were safely down. We had been in the air for over 7½ hours and the F/ E said we had enough fuel left to fill a cigarette lighter. I wouldn't say that crew morale or fatigue were seriously influenced by that single operation, but I think we all realised then that we were into a very tough battle. However, as our tour progressed, there is no doubt that crew morale went into gradual decline as the apparent inevitability of 'getting the chop' wore on our nerves. Crombie started to display irritability bordering on mild hysteria over relatively minor lapses in crew discipline, such as leaving an intercom microphone switched on. Crew members openly talked about 'the chop' and weighed up the chances of survival. In serious moments, one thought dominated our minds: would we, by miraculous luck, somehow manage to get through our tour?

Finally, we are all grateful to Harry for the design of our Squadron Badge. The C / O, Wing Commander A J Sampson, a Newfoundlander, was keen that the caribou should be the principal feature. Fortunately Harry's design won the ballot. Unfortunately Harry was a POW when the approved badge was presented to the Squadron.

Royal approval from HM King George VI for Harry Darby's squadron crest design. It was to be some time before he saw it.

Alan Hounsome, Wireless Operator / Air Gunner

Alan Wireless Operator/ AG Hounsome was a member of one of the first crews to arrive at Foulsham, when 514 Squadron was forming. Being the first crew of B Flight, (A Flight having just been filled) his skipper, F /O David Gray, was promoted to Flight Lieutenant and made Deputy Flight Commander - under Flight Commander Sqdn Leader Roberts. Alan volunteered for the RAF in December 1939, hopefully for aircrew, but was only offered the role of straight (ground) wireless operator, which he accepted. In due course he started service life on 1st August 1940. 'Long and tortuous', describes his path to becoming a qualified aircrew member. Following square bashing, at Melksham, with all the usual spit, polish and bull that went with it, eight of them were posted to a B.B. Squadron. He hoped it might mean 'Big Bomber' or similar, but on arrival at Crewe discovered it meant Balloon Barrage, and each one was sent to a different site. Alan's site was a small piece of waste land surrounded by houses. The only place to wash was a metal bowl outside the guard hut, which he found embarrassing, never having had to carry out his ablutions in public before. The crew comprised a corporal and six men, instead of twelve, which kept them rather busy. Apart from guard duty every other night, the phone rang at least once every hour with a change of alert. The alerts were in colours of red, yellow and green, and for every change, the balloon had to go up, down or to a new height, and every operation would mean calling out the whole squad - which meant nobody ever got a whole night's sleep. Fortunately after six weeks the eight of them were reunited and re-posted.

In the latter part of 1940 a new scheme was started where basic wireless operator training would be given at main post offices. Alan in a party of twenty was sent to Sheffield. They were instructed in the old sorting office by retired telegraphists who taught them well and looked after them well - almost on a grandfather/ grandson relationship, he states. He was sorry when this came to an end at the time of the blitz on Sheffield in December 1940. Back at Blackpool again, and sometime later, he was interviewed by a Sqn Leader and asked what he would think of being aircrew. Even though this was his great desire, he merely replied that he wouldn't mind, and nothing more was said. He only came to realise quite some time later, that he had been accepted for aircrew.

In July '41 it came as a blow to learn that as there were no places yet available on the W/Op aircrew course, he was posted to a maintenance section at 39 M.U. at Colerne. Six months later he was posted to the maintenance section at Hendon. And then an air maintenance course at Cranwell. And so it went, until finally Alan did get his aircrew training and in May '43 Sgt R A Hounsome was on his way to crew up at No 14 O.T.U. (Operational Training Unit) Cottesmore, flying in Wellington's. By the end of O.T.U. he had clocked up 125 hours.

No 1661 H.C.U. (Heavy Conversion Unit) in 5 Group - Lincolnshire, followed, where each crew picked up a Bomb Aimer, Engineer and another gunner, and flying training carried on in Manchesters and Lancasters. Different philosophies held by the Navigator and Alan led to arguments, the Navigator logical, believing that the odds were against them finishing a tour, and Alan fatalistic, believing that no harm would befall him - so the pilot, Sgt Symes, decided for the sake of peace, that one of them should go. Alan volunteered and all remained good friends. Alan re-crewed within a couple of days, joining David Gray's crew whose W/Op had been taken ill. In the event both philosophies were to prove correct, Sgt Symes and crew sadly failing to return from their third operation.

Alan and crew were posted to No 9 Squadron, in 5 Group at Bardney, Lincs on 3rd September '43. There they flew exercise flights and the pilot flew '2nd Dicky' with another experienced crew - his first operation. Apart from operations, Bardney fulfilled a role in supplying crews to certain other squadrons, and after one month there, Alan and his crew mates were posted to 514 Squadron in 3 Group at Foulsham.

Some of the Story of 514 Squadron

On arriving at Foulsham they found 514 Squadron being equipped with Lancaster IIs to which the secret bombing device 'Gee H' was being fitted. To complete training with this new equipment they spent most of the next six weeks blind photographing Ely Cathedral at night. They were allocated Lancaster 'L London' and completed their first operation in her on 11th November - mine laying off La Rochelle in the Bay of Biscay. The Squadron moved lock stock and barrel to Waterbeach on 23rd November '43. All the Gee H equipment was stripped out and they were told that they would be mainly used as Backers Up to the Path Finders.

Alan tells us that one day at Waterbeach, idly watching the flying, one of the Conversion Unit Lancasters taxied up to the end of the runway and commenced take off. Thundering down the runway, suddenly the undercarriage went up and the aircraft belly-flopped down onto the concrete. The rear turret swung round, doors opened, the gunner clothed in a Jackson suit, back somersaulted onto the runway and sprinted smartly away. It appeared that the pilot and engineer had devised a code of signalling to save shouting, especially on take-off. The signal for 'undercarriage up' was for the pilot to raise his right hand, but unfortunately his goggles slipped and he raised his hand to adjust them. The engineer, instead of being aware that they hadn't left the ground, was concentrating solely on the pilot's hand - with expensive results. The gunner thinking that they had crashed, immediately evacuated the turret in the proper manner. This at least settled an argument for Alan and company who had doubted if it was possible for a rear gunner, wearing a Jackson suit, to be able to open the doors and tumble out in an emergency.

Some trips went smoothly, others didn't. Alan's 3rd op on 2nd Dec '43, his second to Berlin, was one of those. The aircraft were required to carry and drop bundles of 'window' on route, 'window' being strips of silver foil (silver paper) of a suitable length, each bundle showing up as a blip on German defence radar screens in similar manner to that of an aircraft. This confused and swamped much of the enemy radar. There was lots of it stored in the rest bed area behind the main spar. The bomb aimer would drop the bundles through a chute at so many bundles per minute, and would call for more as he required it. Alan then had to disconnect his intercom and oxygen, climb over the main spar, reconnect up again and pass parcels to the navigator who would pass them via the engineer to the bomb aimer. Alan then disconnected his oxygen and intercom, climbed back over the spar and connected himself up again. On his second trip over the spar for parcels of bundles, finding the oxygen connection in the dark seemed to take ages. On the third visit for more 'window' he couldn't find the connections at all, so he threw some parcels over with his remaining energy and got back to his normal position as quickly as he could. He was now suffering from severe lack of oxygen, but fortunately the navigator - removing the last packet from under Alan's foot - found him 'out like a light' with his oxygen tube still disconnected. So he connected him up. Alan, hallucinating that someone was disconnecting his oxygen, then disconnected it himself. Being a busy time for the navigator, he called for the help of the engineer. Alan took a swing at him initially, but the engineer restored his oxygen until he once again resumed normality.

The trip to Berlin continued and by this time the target could be seen in the distance. They had a 2nd Dicky with them on this trip (a pilot of a new crew accompanying them for one trip to gain some operational experience prior to taking his own crew on ops). As needs must, the 2nd Dicky went off to the Elsan at the rear of the aircraft. Unfortunately he groped in the dark for a hand-hold and pulled a toggle which was an emergency release for the 7 man dinghy stored in the wing. The dinghy inflated, forced the hatch open in the wing and was swept backwards by the slipstream, taking the IFF (Identification Friend or Foe) aerial with it. All they knew of this, was that the rear gunner reported a large chunk of orange flak passing the rear turret.

Over the target the flak was heavy and they weaved considerably. The skipper set the new course on the D.R. compass for the next 15 minute leg. At the end of this leg they discovered that the compass was faulty - so they were already lost. The Navigator estimated a position and all went quietly for the next hour, then flak and searchlights everywhere and frantic weaving as they thought that they had strayed over a major Ruhr town. Once again a new course was set for the coast, and when the navigator reported that they should be over the sea, they went down to get below cloud in order to get a fix when the English coast came into view. However they were over land and thought they were already over England, so could now break radio silence. The skipper called up Darkie - this being a frequency limited to 10 miles - and an airfield hearing this should switch on its airfield lights. There was no answer but an airfield lit up behind them. They altered course and headed towards it. As they approached the lights went out and another airfield lit up. They altered course again. Alan, suspicious, thought something funny must be going on and tuned into the East Coast Directional Finding Group and tried to get a fix. No luck, they couldn't hear him. So he switched to the West Coast Group, Southampton being their control station. This time lucky, but the position given was only rated a third class fix. The navigator eagerly grasped the fix, although it put them over Paris. Apparently the enemy had been using their airfield lights to lure them into danger. They altered course immediately for the coast, the engineer agitated, being already on the fuel safety limit. Alan warned Southampton of their likelihood of ditching. The pilot tried Darkie again but no luck. The Observer Corps came on, then a master beam came up in the air and then laid across the land, which they followed. A second beam indicated the way. The fuel gauges reading almost empty, they prepared to bale out. Just then Tangmere lights came on and they were already in the approach. Almost on touchdown the engines cut through lack of fuel. For the part he had played in the safe return of their aircraft, Alan was awarded the D.F.M.

Peter Twinn, Rear Gunner

Sgt Peter Twinn was rear gunner in one of the very first crews to join the Squadron. They had already completed 11 operations with No 9 Squadron in 5 Group and were one of three experienced crews from this Group who helped to form the nucleus of the newly forming 514 Squadron. They were posted to Foulsham on 20th September 1943.

His crew, under Sgt Colin Payne, who would later rise to S/Ldr and command 'C' Flight, took part in the first bombing attack by the Squadron on 3rd November, the target being Dusseldorf and also the first operational use of GH. The next five operations for this crew were to Berlin, followed by an attack on Frankfurt on the night of December 20/21, followed by a further five consecutive attacks on Berlin – the last of these being on the night of 15/ 16th February. Many crews who followed later were thankful to have missed such a string of distant and dangerous targets.

Peter further recalls: On 23/24 November the target was, as usual, the Big City but with a difference - on our return we would land at our new base at Waterbeach. How or why it was ever allowed, I never knew, but all kit had to be taken with us! So apart from the full bomb load the fuselage was crammed with trunks, cases, boxes and two bicycles! After six and half hours flying we returned to our new base only to be diverted to Cranfield due to bad weather, arriving at base later in the day. Luckily all the squadron returned but I hate to think what German Intelligence would have made of a crashed Lancaster complete with kit!

The two gunners relied totally on their flying clothing for warmth, unlike the rest of the crew in the heated cabin area up front. On route to Berlin on 15th February, on the leg heading to the north of Denmark, Peter's heated flying suit packed up. These inner suits were wired up like an electric blanket with gloves and slippers attached, the whole suit being plugged into the aircraft's electrical system. Over this was worn the heavy outer suit, leather gloves and fleece lined flying boots. Without the extra warmth from the inner suit, the outer suit could not ward off the cold at -40°C and Peter became progressively colder from the feet upwards. He knew that he should report the suit malfunction to his skipper, but feared that Colin would abort the sortie resulting in the crew having to fly an extra operation. So he said nothing, becoming colder and colder until numb from the waist down.   After completing the trip and a safe landing he found himself stuck in his turret and had to be lifted out by the crew. He recovered shortly, but then faced a dressing down from his captain who knew that Peter couldn't have baled out in an emergency. But in the end Peter was glad that he didn't have to do a further sortie, nor have to face the comments of the crew.

The end of the tour came suddenly - out of the blue! It was a great surprise as the normal tour was 30 operations but we had only completed 26. Several senior crews, ourselves included, who had completed 25+ operations, were informed that their tours had expired. No reason was given except that there was to be a reorganisation of the Squadron. The answer came when we were on tour expired leave - D Day and the invasion of Europe. The Command did not want crews being tour expired and new crews coming in during the invasion period. Consequently we, and the other crews, were posted to training establishments as instructors. So our tour ended on 19th April 1944 after nine months of operations on two different squadrons and flying in two different marks of the Lancaster - Mark I and Mark II. We survived some of the heaviest operations of the war, saw the introduction of the Pathfinder force, new radar equipment and the final buildup of Bomber Command to its peak of efficiency; but none of this was achieved without the terrific cost in aircrew lives. We, as a crew, were lucky. Apart from a few small flak holes and on two occasions we lost an engine on fire and once coned by searchlights, we had a charmed life. We were never attacked by night fighters, although plenty were seen.

A lucky tour indeed but all due to the outstanding skill and leadership of our skipper, coupled with the brilliant navigation of Ken and the professional skill of the rest of the crew. During this period we had all progressed and grown a little older. We had gained promotion and experience.

Geoff Williams, an Australian Rear Gunner, was a member of a crew posted to 90 Squadron at Foulsham in the summer of 1943, well before 514 Squadron came into being. This Squadron flew Stirlings. Sadly their skipper, F/ Sgt D G Evans, Was lost when flying 'second dickey' (pilots usually flew one trip with another crew for initial operational experience) with another crew to Essen.

They returned to Foulsham for the formation of 514 Squadron, their new skipper being S / L E G B Reid, DFC, commander of A Flight. This resulted in their tour of operations taking considerably longer than other crews, from their first operation on 11 Nov '43 to their last on 23 July '44. Targets included five visits to Berlin, and they were fortunate to return early with engine trouble from the Nuremberg attack on 30 Mar '44 when Bomber Command suffered its heaviest losses. Geoff states that of the original 30 crews forming 514 Squadron, only two finished their tours safely. He informs us of the rear gunner's procedure for baling out. The steps were: centralise the turret, pull a trip wire to open the turret doors behind, lie back, grab the parachute pack and clip it onto the front of the harness while still lying back, sit upright then revolve the turret to port or starboard and fall out backwards making sure that the trailing aerial was on the opposite side. Not an easy task when hampered with heavy flying clothing and seconds count.

Fred Brown, Mid Upper Gunner

CREW (514 Sqn Waterbeach, 'B' Flight, 23/2/44-11/5/44)
Pilot P/O A B (Sly) Cunningham RNZAF age 24
Nav F/O R J (Bob) Ramsey 23
B/A F/O R (Reg) Brailsford 35
W/Op Sgt J W (John) Stone
F/E Sgt J F G (Jock) Hay - (not on last flight)
M/U Sgt F W (Fred) Brown
R/G Sgt B L (Taffy) Roberts

Fred, then a sergeant gunner aged 22, now lives in Australia. Extracts from his intriguing story follow. The full version of his account, as of others, will be retained in the Squadron Archives.

May 11th 1944. A day that changed everything in my future life. Air Test. The Cambridgeshire countryside looked great, apple blossom adorning the orchards, sunshine lighting up the meadows. Around the county and back in time for lunch.

Target: Louvain. In the parachute room someone had taken my harness, I was given a very loose one. I complained, John said "Leave it, get it fixed when you get back". Well I had Nancy's silk stockings on, no harm could come to me! On the way in to the target we were coned but managed to slip out of the beams. Over the target, kites everywhere, "Bombs Gone" short dog leg and head for home. A cry from the rear turret. Cannon fire from below the starboard tail plane. Starboard inner already blazing. Feathering and using the Graviner on the engine proved useless, flames now shooting past the tail plane and the kite full of smoke. "Bale Out". To the rear hatch, I rolled toward the tail plane to avoid the flames. Oh what a mistake, the first. I hit the tail plane with my ribs and face, and funnily enough I thought 'Joe Louis couldn't hit like that'. Mistake two, remember the loose harness, when the chute opened it was like a mule's kick in the groin, ever had three lumps in your throat?

Mistake three, I wore loose flying boots, they came off at the same time as the chute opened. The earth came rushing up. I landed in stocking feet, cracked ribs and a face like a squashed pumpkin.

Belgium. I could hear the sound of aircraft returning home, so near yet so far. I had landed in a field, close to a hedge, a ditch running along the hedge, some three or four feet deep. Overgrown and the bottom dry. I hid my gear, parachute, harness and Mae West in the ditch, with a covering of bracken. Not far away, a farmhouse. I took stock of myself nose squashed and bleeding, ribs bruised and maybe broken, crutch pained, my eyes gradually closing and no shoes. I needed help.

I made for the farm, everywhere was quiet. In the farmyard, buildings on three sides, the one on the left had a ladder leading to a loft. I climbed the ladder, bales of hay were stacked in the loft with plenty of loose hay. There was an opening in the floor, through which I could see a storeroom with a door leading to the yard.

About 5.30 I heard movement in the house. The back door opened, a young man, bucket in hand crossed the yard, opened the store room door. He was lifting a wooden lid covering a well, he lowered the bucket, filling it with water. It was now or never, go for broke. I swung on a beam in the floor, dropped next to the young man. He took one look at me, dropped the bucket, screamed and fled into the house. I caught sight of my mirror image in the clear water of the well. No wonder he had thought he had seen a ghost. I could hear raised voices in the house. Two men came across the yard, one about 20, the other a little older. I started saying "RAF RAF RAF" making gestures I had been shot down. They could see, I think, I was aircrew, the younger one put his hand to his lips, be quiet I guessed. They took me into the loft again, sat me behind some bales of hay and left.

After a time, the younger one who I came to know as Guy, brought me a cup of ersatz coffee. The sun shone, the birds sang, I could be at Waterbeach. Then the Flying Forts came over, seemed like hundreds of them, in their tight box formations. I sat and watched, what a sight, those Yanks lifted my morale, all was not lost. I wondered, had Nancy had the telegram, "We regret to inform you..." How would she take the news? (My mother, told my sister Eileen the news when she came home from school at lunch time. Many years later Eileen told me, she couldn't get back to school quick enough to brag about her missing brother).

Guy came back, he made signs, asking where I had hidden the chute. The two men and a girl went searching for it. They came back, asked me again where it was hidden, then came back laughing, to say they had found it. They would pick all the gear up after dark. Guy brought more coffee, the girl brought half a dozen hard boiled eggs. I wasn't hungry, the last thing I wanted was hard boiled eggs. I thought I better show my gratitude, I ate the lot. I showed them I had lost my boots, tore my tapes off showed them the escape photographs hidden under the tapes. I took off my A/G brevet. I was beginning to have confidence in these three. Guy brought more of the foul coffee, and a pair of shoes, too small. I was becoming concerned with my wounds, I could hardly see and my ribs ached. I appreciated the risks these people were taking, for a complete stranger.

After dark Guy returned. I squeezed into the tight shoes, and followed the beckoning Guy down the ladder. Limped across the yard and into a lane, I was to follow some 20 yards behind Guy. I suppose we had walked, limped, 3 or 4 miles. We were at a house, detached with the gate locked. A tall elderly man came out, let us in and quickly locked the gate. Guy knew these people well. The elderly man introduced himself he was Alex Vosier. Later I was to learn, he was a retired gendarme; he had been a sergeant in Brussels.

Mrs Vosier, in her sixties, had a little basic English, so at least I had some contact with them. She said things like "You do will", "You do will sit". She asked, "You do will wash?" Alex boiled a pan of water on the fire.

The water was ready. "You do will undress" What here in the kitchen? I took off my battle dress jacket, then my slacks. I stood there embarrassed, standing in shirt tails and my long johns. An air gunner would have been undressed without his regulation long johns on. "You do will", she made signs to remove my shirt, then the long johns. There I stood, naked, except for Nancy's silk stockings. Roars of laughter. I tried to explain, why I was wearing the stockings, superstition and warmth. I shouldn't have bothered. The story of the Pansy Airman was told many times. Mrs Vosier told it many times whilst I was in her house. The wash, enjoyed by all, except me.

My ribs hurt and my crutch was very bruised and tender. Alex telling him I didn't feel too good. He got in touch with a doctor, one who worked with the escape line. He paid me several visits, strapping me up, saying my wounds would heal in time. Alex agreed to take me (now in civilian clothes) for walks after dark. When out on the road, Alex would talk to me. If anyone passed by, he would poke me, this was a signal for me to answer "Oui, oui". This worked very well, I looked forward to the evening excursions. Mrs Vosier and I played cards, she also gave me the task of grinding wheat kernels into flour. A small grinding machine made my arm ache, but I stuck to the job for hours. Two ladies brought more food, and best of all an identity card and work permit.

My new identity:

Jean Antoine Planque. Born: Courtrai. 3. 3. 1915.
Work Permit. Occupation: Patisser.
Place of work: Gestapo Brussels.

The date of birth was to make me older than I was, apparently, older people were not usually detained. Countries had been bombed recently, the registry office destroyed and with it all the records. I was told, that if stopped for a security check, working for the Gestapo would get me through most checks.

Guy came to see me most evenings, he always brought eggs and rations to help the Vosiers. Guy was a good friend anxious to help. One night Guy brought his girlfriend to see me. She told me they were to be married shortly, her wedding dress would be made out of Guys share of my parachute. I spent hours looking through the chink in the curtains, the same German soldier came around every day, collecting eggs. I watched the Yanks come and go and listened to Bomber Command's four engine beat pass overhead most nights.

Alex received instructions, I was to be moved. Alex told me how to behave on the journey. We walked some distance through the countryside to a tram terminus. Alex spoke to me, I answered with the usual "Oui Oui". I followed Alex on to the tram and sat on the curved seat at one end. Alex paid the fare. Through the outskirts of Brussels, toward the centre. Alex was on his feet, awaiting the next stop (Rouppe Place). I followed, I was on the pavement on a busy road. Alex left, no sign, no handshake, I guess he would be relieved we had not been caught. All I knew about Guy and Alex, was they lived either in Limal or Profondsart. I owed them both, more than I could repay.

I spotted the two ladies on the opposite side of the road. They had been waiting for me. They gave me a sign, follow but do not cross the road. The road was busy, I would hate to get lost now. I was taken to the home of one of them, an apartment. The next day I was taken to a working class area some distance away. I was left with a lady in a two roomed flat. She had several children, just one bed for all of them. The lady told me, her husband had been taken to Germany, she had no idea where, or even if he was still alive. She was very poor, little of anything except sheer courage. She sheltered me for three nights, for no return. I was grateful and humble, she had not only risked her life but also her children's' lives. Another move, this time a teacher picked me up, he spoke very good English. At his home I met his wife and schoolgirl daughter. I shared with them a frugal meal, I hated eating their rations. The schoolgirl was excited about meeting an RAF man. I was doubtful about her being there. Would she talk in school? No room for me to stay at their flat, I was passed to a house to spend the night.

Next day a girl took me to a house close to the centre of Brussels. The house by any standard was palatial. A wide marbled staircase leading to the first floor. I was greeted by a blind lady, tall, grey haired, in her mid-sixties. A charming lady, spoke very good English. She asked if I had eaten. She gave me potato soup. A girl in her twenties came into the kitchen, a courier. She took off her coat, undid the stitches in the lining, took out rolls of bank notes and was on her way. Later I was to find, the blind lady was a fortune teller, a good cover for the comings and goings in the house. I was taken to my room, an attic at the top of the house. The bed was made, blankets all tucked in. I thought I better rest, not much else to do. I pulled the blankets back, to find, in the folds of the sheets, hundreds and hundreds of moth maggots. Great wriggling masses, made me squirm, with my hands I began to squash them, then did my best to scrape them off the sheets. I stripped the bed, remade it, and with the Mona Lisa smiling at me went to sleep. Two days in the room, with little food, and very little contact with the blind lady. On the third morning I was allowed into the kitchen for breakfast. A bread roll and ersatz coffee. Then back to my room, nothing to read, just lie and stare back at Mona Lisa. I was again allowed into the kitchen to share an evening meal. Not having eaten since the morning, hunger pangs never left me.

D Day 6th June 1944 Fast asleep, the bedroom door opened with a bang. The blind lady came in followed by a girl dressed in a maid's uniform, black dress white cuffs. She was shouting, "The Allies have landed, The Allies have landed". I caught their excitement, the blind lady hugging me the maid looking on. Half-dressed, I sat on the bed with them, whilst they told me about the wireless reports of the landings. The maid had been in the house every day I had been there and had no idea I was in the house. My routine never changed, breakfast, then that long wait for the evening meal.

12th June. Mid-morning, the man I had met before called. I was taken to a cafe nearby. A man came and sat beside me, he made signs I should follow him. We were joined by a woman whom he introduced as his wife. Saying his name was Alfonse, he told me we were going to Antwerp. We walked together through Brussels to a road junction. Alfonse stood on the kerb, I thought awaiting to cross the road, but no, he had joined a group of people thumbing a lift. A truck pulled up, its sides and backboard were up, already a few people aboard. The favoured positions, backs to the cab, out of the wind were taken, but Alfonse pushed his way in to get his back to the cab. I was in a comer against the tail board.

We came to Malines, stopped, some got off others got on. Two German soldiers got on, sat close to me. We moved off now there were more troops about, I guessed we were getting close to Antwerp. The truck stopped, an identity check. Two guards checking, others looking on. They started near the cab, Alfonse and his friends first, they handed over their identity cards; a look at the photograph then another look at the man, then the guards gradually moved toward the back. My turn next, a pounding heart, I looked the grey uniformed guard in the eye and handed over my identity card. He looked at the photograph, then at me. He handed back the card without a word and moved to the other side of the truck. My heart was thumping. The fields gave way to built-up areas; this must be Antwerp. Alfonse banged on the cab roof, the truck stopped, Alfonse helped his wife down. I jumped onto the pavement. Alfonse and his wife crossed the road. I followed on the other side, in fact because of the heavy traffic I was unable to cross the road. Alfonse entered a cafe, I crossed the road and followed him in. It was late afternoon, we had a coffee. Alfonse said he and his wife would leave, I would be taken care of by the man behind the counter. I was shown a small store room, cleaning materials, brushes and the like were stored there. A small mattress, I was to stay in this room.

Next morning, I was given coffee and a roll, told to stay in the cupboard. It was late afternoon when Alfonse returned, he said he was taking me to a friend's flat, where I would get a meal. A first floor flat, I was introduced to a couple, both spoke perfect English. The flat, well-furnished and comfortable. I was asked what I would like to drink. Alfonse left, saying he would be back with other British airmen. I was given food, champagne, Alfonse returned with two men, members of the same crew. A Canadian, F/Lt Hayche and his Flight Engineer Johnny Welsh, from Philadelphia, Co. Durham. They had been shot down over Holland on their first operation and had made contact with the Dutch underground. Alfonse left, later three men and a woman arrived; all spoke excellent English.

The Cunningham crew. Back row (left to right): Reg, Fred, Jock Hay, John.
Front row: Taffy Roberts, Sly Cunningham, Bob.

Guy Parys, Fred Brown and Denise Dumont at a presentation to mark Fred's return
to Belgium after 44 years, at Warve Town Hall, June 1988.

Guy and Raymond Parys.

Denise and John Dumont.

Lancasters at Waterbeach

The drinks flowed, two of the men said they would take us on the next leg. Around midnight, two of the men got up to leave, we were to go with them. We had been told during the evening we were to go by truck to France.

Outside a black limousine. The men got into the front seats, we three in the back, Johnny being the smallest in the middle. We began to move, the man in the front passenger seat turned, pointing a pistol at Johnny said, "This is the Gestapo, boys". The thought of baling out occurred, but we were travelling far too quickly to take any action. A short journey, a million things racing through my mind. How do I get rid of my identity papers? What sort of story do I tell them '? Before I had any answers, we turned off the street, through an archway into a well-lit courtyard. We were bundled out of the car into a room so brightly lit, it was dazzling. As we had entered the yard, the driver announced, "Gestapo Headquarters". From being exhilarated a short time before, I don't think I had ever felt so low. Later I was to feel worse, much worse. The others were put in cells. I was to be interrogated.

Fred's story continues with his account of liberation from the POW camp in which he was incarcerated after his capture, described above.

Sunday 22nd April 1945. The previous days, the German Administration had been keeping a low profile. The Russians, we knew, were close to Luckenwalde. We were woken by a bod who had gone to the latrine at first light. He came into the barracks shouting, "THE GOONS HAVE GONE. THE GOONS HAVE GONE". As one man, we made a dash for the doors, he was right, not a German to be seen. Not a goon in a tower, not a goon in the camp. We were delirious in our joy. What would happen now?

The senior officers had already planned for this moment. Within a short time, the gates and offices were manned by German and Russian speaking RAF men. About 7 or 8 am, we heard the sound of gun fire in Luckenwalde and Jutterbug. Then the Russian front line tanks came into sight. One tank came into the camp, the crew waving, then it proceeded to crush the barbed wire around the compounds. We waved and cheered. We watched the front line troops go through, motor bikes and side cars, all sorts of odd transport, no back up stores; these chaps lived off the land. They offered rifles, made signs we should go with them, no one did. In retrospect, I wish I had and been in at the fall of Berlin. Surely an historic event to be remembered.

Only two or three nights previously, two RAF bods had been shot trying to escape under the wire, if only they had waited. The SBO (Senior British Officer) issued an order. No one to leave camp. This for our own safety.

Monday 23rd April. We began to settle down, the euphoria passed. The SBO had taken over and the Orderly Room organised. Forage parties were out, searching for food, fuel, anything that would be of use. A list of tradesmen were called for. I registered as a baker. Well, I had watched Mum bake bread, shouldn't be too difficult, and I wouldn't go hungry working in the bakery.

The Russian troops continued to pass the camp all day, all going toward Berlin. By the afternoon, in spite of the SBO's instructions, private foraging parties were out looking for food. We made a short excursion around the outside of the camp, leaving one of the combine to take care of our belongings. Tomorrow we would venture further.

Tuesday 24th April. Those assigned to the orderly room had found all the POW records. These were distributed to each man, `Personalfarte' (Personal Records). We were given two cards each. The gates were manned by RAF linguists, but we passed in and out of the camp without hindrance. During the morning the Russian Admin types arrived. They assumed control of the camp, took over the admin offices, it was fortunate we had been given our personal records. They issued their first order, "No one to leave camp". Their admin was more bureaucratic than ours or the Germans. Mainly women, all butch types, wearing the same uniform as the men. Next order, "Everyone has to register". This registering was to take some days, we queued awaiting our turn. Name, Rank, Number, age, and home address.

In the meantime, the wire the tanks had crushed was fixed back into position, we were virtual POWs again. A Russian film crew arrived, we were told to line the fence and wave as the camera passed by. This we did with some gusto, but some thought we should have ignored the cameras. I went over to see Sly, he had been out earlier on a foraging party. He along with others had found a field planted with seed potatoes. They had systematically gone through the field, recovered every potato. Sly had finished with 35 small ones, which by the time I had called on him were cooked and ready for eating. Whilst we talked, he ate every last one, skin and all. I didn't expect one, I didn't ask for one, but if offered I wouldn't have said no. Such was the way of POW life.

It looked as though we would have a long stay in the camp under Russian control. There was talk of being sent home via Odessa. By days 3 & 4, several bods had decided to leave, try to make their way to the American lines, somewhere to the South West. We ignored the "Not to Leave Camp" order. We ventured out, foraging, the official parties were doing well, but we wanted to supplement our diet. One day the foraging party brought in a beast, worse for wear than we were, thin, the ribs sticking out like barrel hoops. It was last seen in the kitchen compound.

On our first foraging party, we came across a farm, no damage to the buildings. We walked inside, to find a dozen Frenchmen sitting around the table being served dinner by the farmer and his wife. The French objected to our intrusion. Apparently they had worked on the farm and throughout the war had enjoyed the good life. After threats from both sides we managed to get some eggs. We scoured the barnyard for more eggs, found a few. These were the first eggs we had had since leaving England.

We walked to Jutterbug in the afternoon, just a little to the south. We took coffee to swap, knocked on doors, but the people were too frightened to answer. Russians, mainly women, patrolled the streets in their red uniforms. There were signs of a skirmish in the village, she'll holes in some buildings. Eventually we found a house with a small yard, chickens in the yard, small and skinny, no meat on them, I was for taking them. The old man of the house shook in his boots. Gilly, soft hearted Gilly, felt sorry for him, so we left without the chickens. At one house, our knock was answered. Gilly, who had taken German lessons in Luft VII spoke to them. We offered them coffee, they were delighted. The man, his wife, son and daughter tasted Nescafe for the first time. The eight of us passed the afternoon away, Gilly doing his best, they were pleased we were not Russians. We made our way back to camp, Mike and the others awaiting our booty. We had none, but we had left a little goodwill with a crushed people.

A hidden arms cache had been found in the forest nearby. We explored the area near where the arms had been found, it was great to walk the paths in the pine forest, real freedom. In a clearing we came across a crashed Russian plane, the pilot dead alongside his aircraft. We left him there, for there was little we could do. We found the arms cache, a pit maybe 5 yards by 5 yards and very deep. Bods were digging, finding pistols, machine guns and grenades. Obviously they had been hidden by German troops. I wasn't keen to hang about, if one grenade had gone off, the whole forest would have gone up. We were too close to home to take risks now. There was no advantage in carrying arms.

One expedition I did on my own to Luckenwalde. I came across an old sand pit, full of water. On the bank was an RAF bod fishing, trying his luck with a bent pin. I went over to him, to ask the usual question "Had any luck?" To my surprise it was Donaghue, the F/Lt I had shared a cell with in Antwerp. We exchanged a few words, but I got the impression he wasn't keen on talking to other ranks. I thought `Snobby Bastard, and left. I mentioned the whereabouts of the pond to a couple of army types I met. They told me it had been fished out with hand grenades. I laughed when I thought of that bloke at the end of a line with a bent pin.

On the 28th, we decided to break camp, make for the Elbe. The Russians would not or could not give any news of what was to happen to us. Every day we watched German troops, now Russian prisoners, being marched, trotted, and run past the camp, in utter humiliation. All on their way to Russia. We began to think this would happen to us. So we decided to be our own masters. We packed all we could carry, food, clothes, blankets. We left at first light, leaving Mike Harrington and one or two others behind, they were either sick or felt the venture too risky. Our plan was to head south and then west to the Elbe. We took the railway line out of Luckenwalde that headed south, no fear of trains, all transport had come to a stop. It was a fine day, we felt free and began to enjoy ourselves. By noon we had covered some miles and were in a cutting with a high embankment either side. All of a sudden, we heard and almost felt rifle and machine gun fire, it was close enough to smell the cornice burning. The firing came from just ahead and above us. Had we been exposed we would have copped the lot. Whoever was firing didn't know we were in the cutting. We scuttled to the side of the tracks and tucked into the embankment. We wondered what to do next. Whilst in the cutting we appeared to be safe, the cutting went on for some distance. Could we get through without being seen, should we stay put or go back? After some discussion, we decide to retrace our steps and have another go tomorrow. We had to admit failure. It was late evening when we returned to camp, our floor spots were still free, Mike had kept them for us.

An officer came into the barracks, he called out a list of names, mine was on the list; it was a list of tradesmen required for various duties. I was needed for the bakery. I told the officer Fred Brown had left that day, so now I wouldn't be called again. I was keener to get out of camp than work in a bakery. Next day we couldn't make up our minds what to do, whether to leave or not. I wanted to be on my way. I went into the Yank compound to ask if any of their men were leaving. There was some excitement in the compound, a reporter had got through the Russian lines in a jeep. He was in the Yank orderly room getting a story. A crowd surrounded the jeep, awaiting the reporter to return, I guess I was the only RAF bod there. Whilst we waited, a Yank forced open a box in the jeep, it contained the reporter's rations, chocolate, cigarettes. Much to the disgust of his mates, he stole the lot. I was shocked, taking a man's rations like that. The reporter told us the Yanks were at the Elbe and didn't intend crossing the river. He would report on our living conditions and see if he could get transport to pick us up.

The days passed by, we seemed bogged down. There were skirmishes around the camp, the few Germans were putting up a fierce fight. We heard of the fighting in Berlin, the war hadn't finished yet. Rumours persisted about our release, but it seemed we were to go home through Russia. We listened to the BBC, no need to hide the sets now, enough sets to have one or two in each barrack, sets no doubt taken from nearby houses. We explored the district looking for anything of use. One day we met one of our old guards, he was old, out of uniform now, he had been one of the better guards. We spoke with him, he told us he was living close to the camp, and with luck would miss the trip to Russia.

Late afternoon the 7th May, I was on my usual scrounge, going from compound to compound. I was with the Yanks when a truck pulled in. The first allied vehicle to reach the camp. I stood and listened. The driver was talking to the Yanks. I heard they would be prepared to take a truck load of men back to the Elbe. So without further ado I dashed back to tell Chappie and Co. I told them what I had heard. Did they want to go? They hesitated. I grabbed my Yank greatcoat, left all my other gear and was on my way back to the truck. A friend, Ray Griffiths, had heard what I said, he was with me, hadn't taken him long to make up his mind. We managed to get on the truck, what excitement. Soon we were on the move. In a couple of hours we were at the Elbe, what a welcome sight. There was a temporary bridge across the river, about 200 yards long. After some chat with the Russians and shouts across the river, we crossed and were in Allied territory. The truck took us to Magdeburg, the Yanks had an HQ there.

Tired, happy, but very hungry, we were told that they had a mess at a factory close by. We would be able to get a meal there. Trouble was, when we got there, every liberated POW in the area knew about the mess. We joined the queue that snaked around a large hall, this was going to take a time, the queue moved ever so slowly. It was now late into the night, we could see the kitchen staff working like slaves at the far end of the hall. We just had to be patient, no breaking the line, anyway there was nothing else to do. After a couple of hours we made it to the serving counter, bacon eggs, and ice cream, this was living. Having nowhere to sleep we joined the queue again. The American Quartermaster began to complain, all his rations were going and his staff had to have a break. From the Yanks who were in the queue, he got a reception he wouldn't forget, he continued to serve throughout the night. We eventually got a second serve.

By now it was daylight, we explored the factory looking for a place to sleep. We found one of our old barrack mates, Roberts from Liverpool, he had found a typewriter in one of the offices, said he was taking it home for his niece. We laughed, all we wanted was to get home in one piece. We rested, then took a look round Magdeburg or some of it. We wondered what to do, where to go, there was no organisation to help us. More trucks arrived bringing in ex Stalag IIIA men, we met Chappie and the rest of the combine, just 24 hours behind us. We told them where to get a feed. Chappie had all my gear, he said I didn't deserve it. I agreed, took my diary and POW papers, gave him the rest. That`s the last time I saw Chappie. Had we known, we would have said much more.

Someone told us that there was an airfield at Brunswick, not too many miles away. It was being used to ferry POWs home. Early next morning Ray and I set out to find the airfield. We knew it was to the west. We found the autobahn, no pedestrians allowed, but we walked along the side trying to thumb a lift. Yankee trucks going our way, but none slowed down. Then we realised why, in our ill clad dishevelled state, we looked like refugees. We walked to a turn off, and waited for a truck to slow down on the turn. We shouted at the first truck to turn off the autobahn. It went on then some distance away it stopped; the driver had recognised the accents.

"You English?" he shouted, "Yes," running toward the truck. We told him who we were, what we wanted to do. He and his mates said they couldn't help, but confirmed there was an airfield at Brunswick air lifting POWs. They took a K Pack ration out of the truck, took the cigarettes out and gave us the rest, enough food for weeks. What food, tinned bacon and eggs, chocolate, we fed by the roadside, stored as much as we could carry in our packs. It took a time but eventually we got a lift to Brunswick. We walked to the airfield, it had been a permanent Luftwaffe base, brick-built barracks, every convenience. We reported to a very busy clerk, who took our names, then told us to which barrack to report to. It had been a busy exciting day, we dropped our kit on a bed. I said to Ray, that I would have a scout around see if there was any food going.

In the distance I could see a DC3 being loaded, on the tarmac, a queue of men going aboard. I went to see what was going on. There was a Yank in charge, organising the men climbing aboard. I asked, "How do you get aboard one of these aircraft?" He told me that this was the last flight of the day, all aircraft were full. He then said "If you are an officer, I can get you a flight on this one". It was the quickest field promotion ever. I told him I was an officer. I was told, "You have ten minutes to grab you gear". I flew back to the room, told Ray I had got a lift, picked up my gear and was away. Ray later told me everyone in the room was upset that they hadn't got a lift that night. I was last aboard. I had a position facing the rear hatch, only the rear hatch was not closed. This I was told was a safety measure. It was a hair raising experience, I hung on to the fuselage all the way. We passed over some glorious country, superb scenery. The Yank pointed out the Siegfried Line. I had no idea where we were bound. Late that night we landed on a temporary airfield in Northern France, it was 10th May. On our arrival we were allocated to areas, forms to sit on, coffee but no food. I sat with a couple of army types, they had been POWs for some time. We sat and talked through the night. We were to be shipped out the following afternoon.

In the morning, we decided to have a walk around the village, no point in just sitting and waiting. We carried all our gear with us, didn't want to lose any at this stage. There was nothing of interest in the village, we decided to ask one of the locals to brew us a coffee. A lady answered the door we had knocked on. She invited us in and was about to make a brew of ersatz coffee. We said "No" and gave her a large tin of Nescafe. She was beside herself and had to

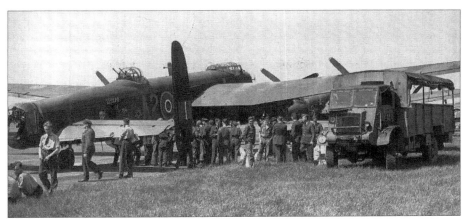

514 Sqn Lancasters took part in Operation Exodus, the repatriation of freed POWs. Eric Brown found himself returning to England in his own squadron's Lancaster a year after he had set out from Waterbeach.

explain to her two young children what it was. The only coffee they had tasted was the ersatz kind. They marvelled at the taste. We thanked them and left them the coffee and all the other rations we were carrying.

Back to the airfield, we had lots of time to kill. We watched the Yanks moving German POWs, this was something we savoured. Some Germans were being loaded onto a big Yankee truck. The Germans complained that there were too many on the truck. My thoughts went back to the crowded cattle trucks. None of us had any sympathy for the Hun. We had all suffered at their hands. The next scene was a delight to watch, especially for this ex-captive audience. The truck driver pulled away along the tarmac, gathering speed, then applied the pneumatic brakes. All those aboard were swept toward the front of the truck, now there was room for as many again. We cheered encouragement to the driver.

Early afternoon we were marshalled along the edge of the runway and numbered off into aircraft loads. In came the Lancasters, squadrons of them, tears came to my eyes. Such a stirring sight. As an aircraft came to rest, a batch of men would board. When it came to our turn, again tears and a lump in my throat, the aircraft letters JI, my squadron. 514 squadron Waterbeach. I spoke to a member of the crew, told him I was 514. He took me up front, I sat alongside the navigator. The deck of the Lanc was numbered, just enough space for each man to squat a number. I was given a spare headset, I passed it to one of the army lads, who would never have heard aircrew on intercom before.

Take off, the French coast, the White cliffs of Dover, Vera Lynn. Tears again. A beautiful day, our destination Ford near Brighton. The date May 11th 1945. I had been away just a year to the day.

Note: RAF parachute silk was heaven sent for wartime brides in occupied Europe. Fred's 'chute was used to make these two wedding dresses by his helpers, and he was delighted to be given one of them, many years later, to pass on to his own daughters as a family heirloom. Fred says that his first helpers are now part of his extended family, as his family is of theirs.

Fred Brown further relates the experiences of his fellow crew members.

Sly, our skipper, had landed on the roof of a café. He had no hope of escape and was captured very quickly. Bob, the Navigator, landed in the Rixensart area. He contacted the underground, was hidden by Josephine Narbond, then moved to Brussels, where one night - the house he was staying in was raided by the Gestapo. Bob was taken POW. The family he was staying with were arrested. Before they came to trial, Brussels was liberated and the family freed.

Reg, the Bomb Aimer, contacted the underground, was hidden in Brussels until the city was liberated. He was back home in the September.

Dereck Winterford, flying as the spare engineer, landed on a railway line close to Limal. A German patrol on the line, taking Dereck for a saboteur, shot and wounded him in the leg. He was taken POW and sent to Luft 3 Sagan.

Taffy, the rear gunner, like Reg was hidden by the underground in Brussels until September. He returned to 514 Squadron, met up with Jimmy Glanville who was getting towards the end of his tour. Taffy resumed flying without any delay. Sad to say, he and the crew he was flying with were killed on Taffy's first op after returning.

John, the W/Op, had quite a story. He landed in the vicinity of Rixensart. He recalls enjoying the drop. He was lucky on landing, his parachute canopy caught the chimney of a tall house, wrapping around the chimney pots. The harness lashed his face, he landed at the side of the house. Freeing himself he left the area with some speed. About half a mile away, he spotted someone, he thought it was me. Someone in dark clothing and what looked like flying boots. To give me a fright, he tapped this person on the shoulder. John was lucky, it turned out to be a very frightened, off duty Gendarme. He took John home, within minutes had burnt John's uniform, and given him some old clothes. John stayed until first light. The Gendarme led the way on a bicycle, took John on the road to Brussels, after a couple of miles without a word he left, leaving John to find his own way. After the war, the Gendarme contacted John.

It was hot, a very hot and sunny day. Passing through Waterloo, John came across a German army camp in the woods. Motorcycle and sidecars were scouting along the roads, presumably looking for shot down airmen.

9 Lancasters had been shot down over Belgium the night before. The patrols, including the dogs in the side cars took no notice of John. In the centre of Brussels, at The Palais de Justice, a German guard turned John back, he was walking into a no go area. Hot and sticky, John made use of the escape money. He went into a cafe, ordered a cup of coffee, spoke to the lady in charge, but he was not offered any help. Then further on, he went into a pub, ordered a beer, the pub was filled with German troops, no one took any notice of John. He headed west and south out of Brussels, heading for France. After starting out at 5am, he reached Halle at 8pm. People sat outside their houses enjoying the late evening. Outside one farmhouse, he watched a man playing with a

frog, making it jump. John thought he looked a reasonable sort of chap. He spoke to him, and later he knew him as Marcel. He was very frightened, but Marcel took him into his house. All the family were home, within half an hour John was in bed. After two hours John was woken. He was interrogated by a man who spoke perfect English, so he should, Fred had been raised in Spalding Lincolnshire. Fred and his wife Molly had been evacuated to England during the first war. Fred was convinced John was who he said he was, and left, saying that Marcel would bring him round to his home in the morning.

Fred's home was the local brewery. Fred was the Brewer. The first day John was hidden on the roof with a very fine view of the country around. Halle was an infantry training centre, John watched the German troops passing by. When dusk came, John met the family, he had the evening meal with them, and was then given a bedroom that overlooked the Mons Road. He stayed in the house for five weeks. One time they had a warning, a warning given on the evening before, that the Gestapo would be searching the area the next day for evading airmen. John was hidden in a basement, part of a disused drain, 4 feet deep, sloping away at a 45 degree angle. Not a nice place, full of spiders, he stayed there all day. He heard the Gestapo searching, they took two boys from next door. They were never heard of again. Molly, who had been evacuated to Leeds in WWI, had lost a lot of weight during Johns stay, from 13st to 8st. She was pleased when John moved to Brussels.

John, taken to Brussels, moved to Clair Debeuster's flat. Later he was joined by two American airmen. Jim Cochrane a Bombardier from Philadelphia and Ray Koch an Air Gunner from Stanford, Connecticut. They hid there for two weeks, then were taken across Brussels to a baker's yard. From the baker's yard, they were taken in the bakers van to Namur, staying the night there. The next day, by truck to Dinart, along the way picking up hitch hikers. One old man who had been picked up guessed who the three were, he gave them knowing winks. All the hitch hikers were dropped at Dinart, leaving the three on the truck. There was an identity card check before crossing the bridge, a sweaty palm job for them. It was relief they were given the go ahead to cross the bridge. On the way south from Namur, the driver had given assistance to another truck that had broken down. He gave the vehicle a tow. Going across the bridge over The Meuse at Dinart the tow rope broke. The Germans at either end of the bridge berated them, telling them to get the vehicles moving. Through all this the three kept quiet in the back of the truck. Later they were dropped and crossed the Semoase river, a ferry boatman taking them over.

They climbed the cliffs alongside the river banks in pouring rain, narrow paths making it a difficult journey. Near Porcheresse, in a forest they found an agent, Mr Robinson. He had a fire going in the pouring rain, no shelter. Mr Robinson brewed coffee, worn out they fell asleep on the sodden ground. Until September, they lived in the forest, making a shelter out of branches. Later they found a disused hut, made bunks with saws supplied by the local people. The local priest, Emil and his sister supplied food occasionally. By the 9th September, when the American army overran the area, there were 30 men hiding in the camp, Americans, RAF and RCAF. The Americans took them back to their base, fed them well before passing them on down the line to Britain.

Seven members in a Lancaster crew, five had asked for help, all had been put in contact with the escape line. That, I think, says a lot for the courage of the Belgium people.

Cedric J Thomson OBE CdeG, Pilot

Crew (ranks at end of tour)

F/O Cedric Thomson, Pilot (Australian)
P/O Ron Cooper, Navigator (English)
P/O Harold Thodey, Bomb Aimer (Australian)
P/O Roy Holdcroft, Wireless Op. (Australian)
Sgt. Gerald Lawrence, M.U.Gunner (English)
Sgt. Derek Gee, Rear Gunner (English)
Sgt. G Wadeley, Flight Engineer (English)

Cedric and his crew were posted to No 1678 Conversion Unit at Waterbeach in April 1944. There were only three crews in each course and they felt themselves lucky to be living at an operational aerodrome with crews already on ops. They trained in this unit from 17th to the end of April. Cedric, then a newly appointed Pilot Officer, relates:

I remember the 'Bulls Eye' to the North German coast in Lancaster II (DS 622), and our last training flight; night tactics with F/Lt Prager. He certainly taught us the extreme limits of the Lancaster II in the corkscrew because our aircraft was put out of action for some time as the ground crew had to replace some fractured parts.

Seven days later we started life in A Flight. On 7th May we went on our first official operation in LL733, 'G' George, under the guidance of F/Lt Chopping. His name did not give us confidence although his guidance was very valuable. The target was Nantes Airfield. We bombed at lower level than most - because we were told to - and bombs raining from above impressed upon us that we were on ops. On our third trip (Courtrai) still in 'G' George, again we were bombing at a lower level - because we were told to do so. I clearly remember a stack of bombs coming at our aircraft from the port bow and the last of them passing me about ten yards away, and reading the word 'FUSED' along the side of the last bomb. Our fourth trip was in the same aircraft on Louvain. On this night we were attacked by night fighters and for the first time put the teaching of F/Lt Prague into use in a very serious way. One of our Squadron aircraft was shot down, piloted by A B Cunningham RNZAF. We had completed four trips in five days. It was an exhausting introduction to operations, but think of the longer hours the ground crews endured in all weathers.

Le Mans followed with fighters again. My notes recorded that we did 35 minutes of corkscrewing. Our first German target was Duisberg. 510 aircraft took part but 31 were lost. My wireless operator's diary called it 'Dante's lnfemo'. A loss rate of 6. 1% was too high. 514 lost three aircraft. Having a very accurate bomb aimer we went round the target twice, each time a few thousand feet lower in order to avoid oncoming aircraft. The second time round I made it quite certain that we were not going around again! In late May we went to Boulogne twice and in between we went to Angers which took 7½ hours.

June began with the D DAY landing. I remember that all aircrew were given revolvers to wear. Then we briefed in the evening of the 4th, but shortly afterwards the trip was delayed whereupon the station was closed and the RAF Regiment deployed their troops around the aerodrome preventing anyone leaving. We all guessed that the raid was part of D DAY attack as we had never seen so many senior RAF Officers at a briefing before.

ln addition we noticed that all aircraft had black and white stripes painted on their wings and we had never been on a trip when the target was to be bombed at dawn. We were not told that this trip was the invasion but that if we saw a large number of aircraft and ships around we weren't to be surprised. Twenty one 514 aircraft took part. After final briefing and a flying supper of greasy eggs and bacon, we took off at 0335hrs, set course at 0409, and crossed the coast just east of Beachy Head at 0435. We crossed the French coast at

0507hrs and bombed a minute later at Ouistreham where we destroyed some gun emplacements. We turned east round Le

Havre and crossed the coast at 0526hrs on the way home. We were privileged to see a massive display of ships of all shapes and sizes and a huge number of aircraft including gliders being towed. The gunfire on and around the beaches was spectacular.

The next night we went to Massy-Palaiseau, railway marshalling yards, near Paris. This was heavily defended and on our return we were attacked by fighters. Two aircraft from 514 were lost, flown by P/O McGown and F/O Greenburgh. The casualty rate was remaining high. Ten days later we went to Montdidier, again railway yards. That was the last time I flew a Lancaster ll.

The great day arrived when we were allotted a Lancaster III (PB142) 'A' Able. We were given the first dispersal point near the end of the main runway facing the Cambridge - Ely road. This aircraft was equipped with H2S radar which was entirely new to the crew. Each time we flew we learnt more about H2S. We went on a mixture of German targets and VI launching sites and later V2 sites followed. There was even a V3 site. In between there were targets to assist with the Army front line. On the 30th June we bombed Villers Bocage where the army was closing around the enemy. Two out of three aircraft lost were from 514. Although we were bombing fewer German targets than in the winter of 43/44 the chop rate was still fairly high. The enemy fighters were very strong and well organised. Nevertheless we bombed seven targets in July. The last one in that month was to Stuttgart which took 8.10 hours. This trip had everything, searchlights coning us, fighters all the way home, heavy flak over the target, and going around again at the target. The crew were most efficient throughout and the two gunners kept the fighters at bay. The running chart of Ron Cooper on this trip is displayed at the RAAF School of Navigation at East Sale, Victoria, so the flight of one aircraft of 514 is honoured in a far off place.

Cedric and his crew also took part in a special attack on a building in France. This was carried out by a lead Mosquito and two Lancasters. The differing aircraft speeds caused formating problems but they accomplished the task, bombing from about 2000 feet. On another occasion the outward flight to a target near Paris was not much above ground level, as they were instructed not to fly above 150 feet over England. The first part of the route was to Lands End and Cedric recalls looking up at cars at one time, as this force of 100 plus Lancasters careered along the Cornish valleys. They continued at low level over the sea to the west of Brittany, crossing the French coast further south, and eventually climbing in the dusk to at least 20,000 feet as they approached the target. The ruse may have avoided radar detection on the way to the target but fighters were around after they had bombed.

About this time three of his crew were commissioned and Cedric was able to enjoy their company in the Officer's Mess. On 7th August they attacked enemy troop concentrations on the Caen front. It involved bombing at night, at a lower level than normal, just in front of our troops who sent up Very lights to mark the front line. On return, Cedric was told to go to London that morning by train where he was met and taken to the BBC to be interviewed for a War Report covering this attack. Cedric enjoyed the experience, meeting John Snagge and others, and returned on the midnight train; some 44hours of very little sleep for which he subsequently received £9.9.0 from the BBC.

Cedric recalls fighter affiliation (combat practice) with an American Mustang. Afterwards the Mustang swept over the aerodrome very low and then went vertically upwards into cloud. A few seconds later the aircraft fell to the ground. It seemed an unnecessary death.

On 20th July their target was a night attack on the synthetic oil plant at Homberg, heavily defended with flak and fighters. They were hit by flak in the fuselage and elevators. Losses were heavy, including four from 514 Squadron. Other difficult targets were Bremen, Russelsheim, and unexpectedly some of the French targets. Cedric states that other crews had similar or worse experiences, especially those flying in the winter of 1943/44.

One evening at dusk the first aircraft at take-off raised its undercarriage too soon and with full bomb and petrol load skidded along the runway on its belly, stopping with it's nose hanging at the edge of the Cambridge - Ely road. The bombs on this operation had time fuses which once set could not be defused. All other aircraft took off but as the cloud level was already about 1000 feet and drifting down, all were recalled before reaching the coast. They were ordered to reduce landing weight by jettisoning fuel and then to discharge their bombs on a disused bomb practice site. All aircraft eventually landed and taxied to their dispersals. As Cedric's dispersal point was close to the main runway where it adjoined the Cambridge road, they were instructed to stand by as the fixed fused bombs were removed from the damaged Lancaster and transferred to theirs. When fully loaded they took off into the lowering cloud base and flew to the Wash where they dumped the bombs with twenty minutes to spare before some were timed to go off.

Cedric concludes: We finished our tour in September 1944. During our time the Squadron lost 34 aircraft which is more than the Squadron numbers. I am very proud to have led an above average crew, all who contributed to our survival and achieved a measure of success in our tour. It was very pleasing that the crew were recognised by the award of the Croix de Guerre, with Silver Star, which I am pleased to hold on their behalf I was twenty years of age and the last full gathering was at Lyon's restaurant in London to celebrate my 21st birthday, and to say goodbye.

Corporal 'Mel' Melluish, Armourer

E 'Mel' Melluish, corporal armourer, was in the RAF pre-war. Apart from serving in a little known unit of RAF armoured cars in Iraq, he also had operational experience early in the war when many of us were still at school. 'Mel' relates:

I had experienced the anxieties and nervous tensions that build up inside whilst attending briefing, and the journey out to dispersal, putting on an air of bravado and hoping that the tenseness wasn't too obvious. Although a tradesman on ground crew, it was then a common thing for the armourer to take on the duties of air gunner on a plane that he serviced. When war was declared this obligation was carried out without question. I was rear gunner on a Mk.I Whitley, in a manually operated turret with one gun. I had carried out 9 operations when in early 1940 it was declared that all aircrew would be granted the rank of not less than sergeant. It seems it was noted that owing to the number of tradesmen that were involved in flying duties there was a lack of skilled men to maintain the servicing of aircraft, and it was quicker to train an air gunner than the trades required for the maintenance of planes. So tradesmen such as myself were taken off flying. I admit that I was very much relieved.

Mel recalls the booze-ups that crews put on for the armament staff, and also taking part in the crazy drinking sessions of 'Cardinal Pouf in the Brewery Tap opposite the main gate, when the skippers of crews, celebrating completion of their tour, were held up to put their signature on the ceiling with the smoke from a lighted candle.

Bob Armit, Air Bomber

Bob Armit in happy mood.

Pilot: Sqn Leader D.W.A. Stewart

The fifth of June 1944 seemed to me just like any other day on the squadron at Waterbeach. Our crew had been detailed on three operations during the last week of May, but strangely, nothing in the last five days. The weather had not been too good during that time, although I would not have thought that it was all that bad. Today was much more like a summer day and I was lounging on the grass outside the flight hut with a cigarette and the dog-eared daily paper when our mid-upper gunner came over and sat down beside me.

"We are on tonight, Junior..." he said quietly. "Briefing is at a quarter past one!"

"That's a bit early in the afternoon," I answered. "It must be a blooming long one. Any idea where gunners going?"

"No idea. And it's in the morning!"

"Crikey! Briefing half past one in the morning .... we will just about be airborne when the sun comes morning will be like doing a daylight."

Briefing didn't seem the same as usual. The various officers that came onto the dais and said their own particular piece seemed to be energised and bubbling and yet somehow vague. Instructions at times were not as specific as they were normally. The target was to be Ouistreham which was right near the French channel coast.

There were no details of any precise aiming point or what the quarry would be. The navigator would tell us en-route. Our operational height was to be ten thousand five hundred feet. This was pretty low. We would normally go in at twice that height.

My job as the air bomber during the journey to and from the target was to try to obtain visual fixes by map reading, that is, if it was possible to see the ground. I collected my maps which were issued at briefing and were only enough to cover the route. I pencilled in the route and realised that the only map reading that I would be able to do would be over Blighty. This certainly seemed to be a piece of cake. Take off was to be at 03.45 am. Over the channel I concentrated on checking the sky for fighters. We must have been about ten or twelve miles out from the French coast when I saw a small break in the cloud showing a circle of dark, dark sea. As it passed beneath the aircraft, just slightly to port, I wondered what the white spots were. I looked hard at it and then realised that they were not spots, but more like tadpoles and were the wakes of a flotilla of small boats, all on a zig-zag course. Then it was gone. The gap had closed. I was about to switch on my intercom to ask if any others of the crew had seen them, when it dawned on me that this was an invasion fleet. That would explain a lot of things. I still thought, in my excitement, that

I would tell the lads and give them something to cheer about, but my second thought was that if we got shot down, and survived, then Jerry would have seven of us as a possible source of information. So I kept quiet.

A few minutes later the navigator gave the pilot the details of the time and distance from the target, and he started to lose height gently to come down through the cloud. It was my clue to start to get things organised for the bombing run. As we broke cloud I looked around to see where we were and spotted two ships slightly ahead and to port and assumed that they were just rounding the headland from Le Havre. They would make a good target, I thought, but a heck of a job to hit them from this height. However, it seemed that someone down there had exactly the same thoughts about us, for as I looked at it the whole of the deck of one ship started to twinkle as they opened fire and the flak started to climb slowly, slowly up towards us. It came slowly closer and closer, then suddenly appeared to change speed and shot past us like an express train. By the time that the first shots were closing in the second ship had opened up on us too. The skipper did not need any advice from me about evasive action. "I'm going back up" he called over the intercom and as he said it the nose of the Lancaster lifted as if in disdain and within seconds the cloud enveloped us again.

By now we were too close to the target to stay up in cloud. We dropped down below once more by which time the flak ships were paying attention to someone else. This was the moment when all my thoughts had to be concentrated on the shoreline. My mind started to rapidly take in the detail. The first thing, of course, was to see where the flak ships were, so I looked east into the wide mouth of the river Seine but could not see them.

My gaze followed the coastline slowly towards the west searching for a suitable target. The navigator told me that this was what we would do a little earlier. I became somewhat puzzled as I looked along the beaches a little to starboard because they seemed to be obscured by a parallel line of fog or smoke. I followed this along to the western end where I saw, protruding from the smoke, bow first, almost the whole of a major warship, with all guns firing at the shore. A closer look at the scene showed that there were another four or five other warships within the smoke, in line astern, and all firing at the beaches as fast as they could load. It was an incredible sight but no time to watch it, even though it took only a few seconds. It had to be back to the business in hand. We were so close to the coast that it was imperative to pick a target so that I would have enough time and distance to manoeuvre onto it for an accurate run. It was not a good idea to go around again, for I would not be popular with the rest of the crew.

Slightly to port I picked out a river, or canal, which ran into the sea through a series of locks and I thought that that would be appropriate. I gave the pilot directions for a turn to port and then a gentle turn to starboard so that we were running up to it quite nicely. It needed only a small "Left ..... left..." to bring the aircraft square onto it. "Bomb doors open..." Straight and level for a few long seconds. "Steady...steady..." and the approach was good.

I pressed the bomb tit just ahead of the locks and the first bomb exploded in the sea, dead in line. The second was just in front of the first lock gates and the next was spot on target. The rest went straight down the waterway. I was exhilarated by the success, and have often wondered since how useful that was to the oncoming battle. We carried on straight and level long enough to get a photograph and then did a gentle climbing turn to port, up into the cloud again and onto course for base.

We landed at 06.37 am. With everything switched off we gathered our kit and climbed out, walked a short distance from dear old 'G' George, sat down on the grass and lit a cigarette while we waited for the crew bus. The first cigarette was sheer bliss!

Back at the briefing hut we collected our mug of coffee and tot of rum, and waited for a table to be free for our de-briefing. It was soon our turn and it was at this moment that I decided to tell what I had seen on the sea and on the target. Standing behind our Intelligence Officer was a tall Squadron Leader who never spoke at all during the session but took a keen interest in everything that we had to say. After our de- briefing was completed, as we started to walk away, he came over to me and asked me to repeat what I had seen. He then asked my name and where I lived. And that was that. I must say that I wondered, with some trepidation, what it was all about. But now it was bacon and eggs and straight into the pit.

On my way to the mess before lunch, one of the lads saw me wandering along and shouted out "Hey, Junior you are in the paper!" He told me that I had got myself in the Times. With almost complete disbelief, I had a little chuckle and carried on to the mess. I found the Times and saw it on one of the inner pages as he had said. That Squadron Leader this morning was obviously a war correspondent, and this was his story. With the usual reporter's flair for making the items sound better, he had put me in as being the first man across. I laughed but was very pleased to accept the accolade.

Forty five years later, on the anniversary of that event, the Times produced a souvenir print of the 6th June 1944, but it was obviously a later edition. As more facts had come in on that day, and the story had begun to fall into place, so I could no longer be the first man across. I didn't mind, but it had been lovely while it lasted. I have been to the Newspaper Museum at Colindale to see if that first edition is on file but no such luck, and now I don't suppose that I shall ever see again that version where I was the first man across on 'D' Day.

BOB ARMIT in happy mood

N.B. In his accompanying letter, Bob commented: 'Well never mind! I was at least first across in our Kite!

Eric Basford, Engine Fitter A Flight

Eric has drafted many interesting accounts of life and background at Waterbeach, the first extracts of which appear here. Other extracts follow later.

33 Base. My arrival at Waterbeach in November '43, to join 514 Squadron, coincided with a large scale reorganisation of No. 3 Group of Bomber Command. A new concept of 'the Bomber Base' was being introduced. A base was to comprise three stations (or airfields) each of which would house a heavy bomber squadron. One of these stations would become 'the base station' and an Air Commodore, appointed AOC the base, would be resident there. Each 3 Group squadron was being expanded to have three flights, A, B and C, instead of just two Flights.

Waterbeach had already been designated as base station for No 33 Base when 514 Sqn moved in, two days before I arrived. The other two stations in the Base were closer to Ely: Witchford with 115 Sqn and Mepal with 75 New Zealand Squadron, Similar arrangements were being set up throughout 3 Group, but I am not sure whether other groups in Bomber Command were doing likewise. I do know that 5 Group (South Lincs) still had two-flight squadrons in 1945. ,

Servicing. A Base Servicing Unit was already being set up in one of the hangars at Waterbeach. This unit, independent of the three squadrons, was to deal with extensive repairs and major inspections on aircraft that had been detached from the squadron. What was previously Maintenance Flight on each squadron became known as R & I (Repair and Inspection) Flight. The Base Servicing Unit relieved the new R & I Flights of much major servicing work, but in turn the R & I Flights were allocated the task of minor inspections at 50 flying hours, 100 hours, 150 hours etc. plus repairs expected to take three days or more. This resulted in the workload on the ground crew of each aircraft in

Engine fitters such as Eric Basford often had to work outside in inclement weather, and were expected to keep their charges airworthy under extremely difficult circumstances. Although this photograph was taken at RAF Woodbridge, the aircraft in the background is 514 Sqn's LL624, JI-P.

the flights being reduced, along with that of the other specialists involved, e.g. electricians, instrument repairers, armourers, etc. Previously they did the minor inspections and repairs besides the daily servicing routines. It meant that minor inspections would be completed in the relative comfort of a hangar, instead of outdoors on the dispersals where the vagaries of the weather often created problems. That was the theory. It needed some 'give and take' in practice at times, but it worked reasonably well. The concept of a regular ground crew for each aircraft in a flight and the responsibilities of the ground crew for their aircraft did not change in any way. A flight sergeant, universally referred to as 'Chiefy', remained as NCO I/c Flight.

Unauthorised flying: if any member of a ground crew wished to fly in one of the Squadron's aircraft (usually his own) there was an official procedure to follow. Assuming that the pilot agreed to take him on a particular flight, his name would be recorded as being on the flight and he would be issued with helmet, oxygen mask, parachute and harness for the trip. In spite of this facility, it was not unusual for ground crew members to persuade their pilots to take them along unofficially, if the flight was only for an hour or so. That meant foregoing the helmet and parachute, but that was the price of short cutting official procedure. As no serious attempt was made to stamp out such unofficial flying, it was assumed to be acceptable practice.

However, unofficial flying over this country in daylight (on officially approved flights) was one thing, but to do it at night and beyond our coastline was something else. But one of our flight riggers did, on the night of 1st May 1944 when his A Flight Lancaster was scheduled to do a 'bullseye'. This was a rare task for the Squadron, as they were usually undertaken by crews nearing the end of their OTU or Heavy Conversion courses. Bullseye were diversionary tactics designed to irritate the enemy defences, and involved flying towards one of the channel ports or coastal towns of Europe. Then, having alerted the defences, the spoof raider would turn for home whilst still out of range.

On this occasion, the aircraft failed to return and it was revealed by another member of the ground crew that the rigger, Aircraftsman G Robinson, had been aboard. Whether he had been equipped with parachute and Mae West will never be known, but neither he nor the air crew survived. The eight names appear in the 514 Squadron book of memory in Waterbeach church, and in the memorial book for No 3 Group of Bomber Command in Ely Cathedral.

Harry Osborn, Flight Engineer

Sergeant Harry Osborn was a Flight Engineer, aged 20, who served on the Squadron from April '44 until the night of 15/ 16th June '44, when he was killed. During his time on the Squadron he wrote a personal account of his first operational flight, reproduced here:

MY FIRST OP by Harry Osborn.

It was on the morning of Saturday, the 22nd of April, 1944 that my report begins, the time being about 10 o'clock. Myself and the rest of the crew were all standing around in a group outside the flight office chatting, while we were waiting to see what we had been detailed for that day. We had heard that there were ops on that night but we did not know if we would be on the battle order, we would not know until 10.30. At last we saw the skipper coming from the Flight Commander's office, yes we were detailed to fly, this was to be our first op. It gives you a peculiar feeling when you are first told, I would not say so much fear as of curiosity and expectancy, although I must admit I was a bit scared but then the rest of the chaps are feeling the same so you don't worry about it.

The next thing on the programme was to check the aircraft over and give it a Night Flying Test (NFT). The gunners were cleaning and checking their guns while the pilot and myself test the oxygen, intercom, saw that fire extinguishers and oxygen bottles were in position, also that the aircraft is not damaged in any way etc. Then we went up on test, this is to see that the kite flies OK and to check a few other things while in the air. After this came dinner. After dinner we got what things we would be needing for the trip and then got in a few hours' sleep. Tea was at 4.30 and at 5.25 or 17.25 hours the Navigator and Bomb Aimer had to report for Pre-briefing. The Skipper is not allowed into their briefing until half an hour after the start. While they were doing this I had a bath and shave, and got changed into my flying underclothes.

Lancasters at Waterbeach

At 1955 hrs we had our flying meal. This is quite some turn out, the boys arrive in all manner of queer get ups, the most striking thing being the assortment of different coloured scarves, others have civvy shirts, white roll top polo jerseys, flying boots on and an assortment of good luck charms. In fact to see them one would think that they were going to a Sunday School treat rather than a raid. The meal consisted of egg, bacon and chips and as much bread and butter as you wished for. At 20.35 we all had to report for main briefing. Here we have all the crews that are taking part in the night's operation, navigators are plotting the courses on their maps and writing down winds. There is the C.O. of the Squadron, the Group Captain and a host of other officers of the various sections. Then the C.O. takes the platform and we hear that so commonly known phrase "The Target for Tonight". Our particular target being 'Dusseldorf'. Next the Met. Officer gives the gen on what the weather will be like, height of cloud, the temperature where icing is likely to be encountered etc. Next the Intelligence Officer says his part, when the target was last bombed, what we are after hitting, type of defences liable to be met, if any other raids are going on. Then the C.O. tells us what speeds and height to fly, at what wave of bombers we are in, fuel load, bomb load, time of take-off, time to set course, time over target.

After briefing we collect our flying rations and walk over to the cloak room to get our flying kit and get dressed. Here we have a Medical Officer and he gives us two wakey wakey tablets to take before we reach the target, also he has an ointment which the gunners smear on their faces to prevent host bite. At 9.25 or 21.25 hrs transport arrived to take us out to the aircraft. Then the pilot and myself make a final check on the aircraft, while the Wireless Operator tests his set. The boys then lay around smoking and chatting till 10.30 when we all get into the kite and start engines and then give them a run up. We then taxi out to the runway ready for take-off. We got the green 'Go' from the caravan and took off at 10.50 or 22.50 hrs. We then had to circuit round the drome for 40 mins before setting course and at last we were on our way.

As we neared the enemy coast we were all on the lookout for fighters and other bombers in the stream. We crossed the coast at 20,000 ft. As we flew on towards the target we started to see a few searchlights and bursts of flak. Every now and again we would see fighter flares also a few scarecrows. These come up at you in the form of a small ball of fire, then it would burst throwing out showers of sparks and clouds of black smoke which gives it the appearance of an aircraft which has been hit. As we came into the target area we could see the vapour trails of other aircraft and sometimes the aircraft themselves as dozens of searchlights were now searching the sky. Every now and again we would feel a bump in the aircraft as we would be caught in the slipstream of another kite or some flak burst near us. Just ahead of us lay the target lit up by fires caused by the bombers before us, also by flares and hundreds of incendiary bombs. We could now see the marker flares dropped by the Path Finder boys, so we started to make our run up on the target. Here we were cornered by about half a dozen searchlights so the Skipper took a bit of evasive action and we had soon shaken them off At 01 .02 hrs we dropped our bombs and now we were flying straight and level over the target so that we could get some good photos. It seemed hours before the bomb aimer said OK photos taken, this was because we had been caught again in the searchlights, but now at least we were heading for home. You feel as if you just want to sit back and relax but you know there are fighters to contend with so you keep a good look out for them.

As we neared the Dutch coast the Skipper said the kite was handling badly and she was pulling round to starboard. So I made a check on the gauges and found that the oil pressure had fallen off the gauge and also the boost and R.P.M. had dropped considerably so I had to feather this engine; that was at 02.03 hrs. Later I found out that the main bearing had gone on this engine, so we flew the remainder of the trip home on three engines.

As we came near the English coast we could see searchlights flashing and they certainly gave you a feeling of relief The Skipper decided that we would land at an emergency 'drome, this 'drome has an especially long runway and is for all aircraft to land on when in trouble. So we called them up and asked them if we could land. They told us to go ahead and that transport would be waiting for us at the end of the runway.

The Skipper made a really wizard landing and the transport was already waiting to take us to the medical room where we were given rum. Next the Skipper and myself were taken to a hut where we had to make out a report on what was wrong with the kite. Then we were all taken down to the cookhouse where we were given fried egg, bacon and chips, after this a place to sleep and we certainly did appreciate that bed that night. Next day we were picked up by an aircraft from our own Station and flown back to base. Here we had to go for interrogation where we were asked all sorts of questions, and at last our first operational flight had come to an end, resulting in slight damage by flak and one engine U/S. (unserviceable)

The other crew members who flew with Harry Osborn were:

Pilot C F Prowles
Nav A H Morrison
B / A R B Spencer
W / Op R Surtees
R/ G A A Holmes
M / U / G J Porrelli

The only survivor, on the night of 15 / 16th June 1944 was the Navigator, an Australian named Arnold Morrison, who wrote the following letter on 11th November 1944.

Dear Mr & Mrs Osborn,

I have just received your letter and was very disappointed that it had not arrived a little earlier. You see I have been repatriated to Australia, and at this stage of proceedings, I will not be able to come and see you. I wanted to come before and also see the parents of the rest of the lads but Air Ministry would not give me all the addresses - why, I don't quite know. I guess that you are anxious to know just what happened to the lads, and I want to tell you, as nearly as I can remember, all the facts.

We had, as you know, bombed the railway marshalling yards at Valenciennes in the north of France. We hit the target very solidly, as usual, having an A1 bomb aimer, and had turned for the run out of the French coast. It was a very dark night with no light at all below us and just a very small amount in the northern sky.

Ted, the pilot, said that there was a small layer of cloud just above us then, and he was going to climb just above it so that the gunners would have some little reflected light from the clouds to assist them. Just then a night fighter, which must have been following us for a fair while, opened fire and hit us in the port wing (the left hand one, looking forward). Ted took immediate action to avoid it, but he had hit us too hard and the whole wing was a mass of fire. Ted then said that he could not maintain height, and said 'Bail out chaps. I'll see you later'. Harry helped Ted on with his chute, and then put his own on. I put my pack on also and stood behind Hairy. Meanwhile, the bomb aimer was struggling to get the escape hatch open and then he turned around and looked up at us with his palms upwards, telling us that it was jammed - apparently by cannon shells, or splinters from them. We were then very low and losing height quickly and the fire was getting worse, and we realised that we hadn't much chance. Ted, Harry and I looked at each other and gave the thumbs up sign - our farewell. Then we hit the ground and all I remember is a red flash in front of my eyes - I didn't feel any pain and I'm quite positive that Harry and the rest of the lads did not feel anything either. I don't know how I escaped with my life - I had only cuts and scratches and a slight concussion. I woke 2 hours later, right in the middle of a field, and set out to find the other lads, but because of the concussion, I was very light headed and wandered around until daylight, when there was no sign of the aeroplane.

The people of Croiselles turned out in large numbers to provide a funeral with full honours for the crew members of DS816.

The French people I met later told me that the lads were given a beautiful funeral, and 2500 people attended. They were buried in the British cemetery at Croiselles, in the Pas de Calais. They held a special mass in Arras Cathedral also, for our lads, and the same number of people came to pay their last respects and tributes. I was gratified that the last observances on the chaps who were my best friends, were carried out by the wonderfully grateful and very kind French people. They were, I think, as grief stricken as I was about the lads' deaths - their regard for the lads or the RAF was really something wonderful to see.

I hope that this story has not upset you both too much. I shall never completely lose the sense of loss that I have had since it happened - I know that I shall always feel proud to have flown against the Hun with Harry and the other lads - they were as fine a crew as the RAF has produced - they were thought very highly of by the Wing Commander - he had complete faith in them.

I honestly think that Harry was the coolest member of the crew. On our first trip - to the Ruhr - we ran into some trouble and had to come home on 3 engines, and Harry's prompt and efficient handling of the matter undoubtedly saved us from having an engine on fire. He was always such a great source of help to the pilot, particularly during landings, that Ted never had to worry about or question the engine settings etc., and believe me that was very important.

Well, dear friends, that's about all. Would you write to me at my home address (in Canley Vale, NSW, Australia) and if there is anything else I could tell you I will gladly do so. I would like to hear from you very much.

Cheerio for now and may God be with you always.

Arnold Morrison

Bernard Yeomans, LAC Fitter II E

Bernard pleasantly recounts the skilled maintenance work that went on unceasingly: I was very much on the periphery of 514 Squadron, although very much a creature of Waterbeach, being there from about March 1942, to August 1944.

I came to Waterbeach as a very new FM / E straight from 3 S.of T.T., Squires Gate, Blackpool, to be met by this huge aircraft, built like a block of flats, a Stirling of 1651 H.C.U. Nothing I had been taught on the FM/ E Course had prepared me for this shock to the central nervous system. My only physical experience with aircraft had been with a very dilapidated Westland Wapiti, minus wings, fabric, tail plane, rudder, plus a very asthmatic Pegasus Engine, which could be coaxed into life with several attempts on the 'inertia starter', a lot of sweat and the help of another FM / E with a strong arm. This Aircraft had last seen active service on the Indian North West Frontier.

Within a few months I had developed the abilities of a chimpanzee and the skill of a budgie being able to tie engine covers on hanging upside down, in a Force 6 Gale. Absolutely nothing could be done engine-wise from the ground. With all this skill now at my finger tips and being able to 'till up' without disappearing over the trailing edge, on a frosty winter night, the 'powers that be' decided such skill should be rewarded, so I was sent to Innsworth Lane, Gloucester for a Fitters Course, completing it and being sent back to Waterbeach, only to find the 'Pterodactyls' of the aircraft world had flown away to West Wratting and I was posted to the 'new unit'. So begins my relationship with 514 Squadron. I was assigned to 33 Base. Exactly what the relationship between 514 Sqn and 33 Base was, no one ever explained. I think the relationship between them with the 'Rings' and those with the 'Stripes' and 'Props' was covered by the 'official secrets act' carried to the ultimate degree.

Arriving at Waterbeach, again, in late November 1943, to find tradesmen arriving by every train, bus and lorry. Knowing my way around I soon found an empty bed in my old billet. I was assigned to 'B' hanger, to find a hanger full of unassembled trestles. With so many bodies now at the NCOs command, the physical assembly soon got underway. The hanger was under the command of Sqd/Ldr Pearce and W /O Blackmoor. What started as bodies arriving from 'Four Corners of Empire, in a chaotic mass, soon developed into a very good shift system. The hanger was manned 24 hours a day, 7 days a week, with three shifts, two shifts on 5am until 10pm, or 5pm on alternative nights, one shift 10pm until 5am. A 36 hour 'Stand Down' at the end of the third week.

Outside the hanger brand new Lancs arrived direct from the Ministry of Aircraft Production, which were hauled into the hanger, mods checked and / or were fitted, flare chutes for example. At one period we were receiving 30 new aircraft a month, these were sent to Witchford and Mepal as well. During the nine months I served in the Hanger Mk Is, IIs and IIIs came through for various mods. With the Mk IIs came the familiar Hercules Engines I had worked on in the Stirling.

In the summer of 1944, when ops were on, we would stop work, collect at the door of the hanger and wave the aircrews off, 'Wishing them Well' and hoping our Work would stand them in good stead. A few WAAF also knew 'Take Off Time' and stood alongside us, which I thought was very poignant and very moving.

After 'D' Day the aircraft replacement wasn't so acute and there was a general turn down in the number of new aircraft arriving. Most of my contemporaries were notified of a future posting, the majority of single men for the 'boat', the married men posted to Locking for conversion into sailors for the Fleet Air Arm.

I sailed for India on 1 November 1944, and spent two years in a very large maintenance Unit, 322 MU, Cawnpore, Central India, whose main occupation was maintaining aircraft carrying supplies into Burma. These were major overhauls, engines out, complete rebuild, to maker's standards. From India I was repatriated to become a civilian again.

I met Hugh (Woodcraft) at the 1996 Reunion. Just very briefly, we walked off the car park together, didn't know him from Adam. I wrote him a similar letter to this and he very kindly invited me to the next reunion after I had seen the brief statement in the 'Airmail' asking for 514 Squadron members to write in. So, sadly, I never met the 'Heart and Soul' of 514 Sqn, the men that flew the Lanc and the people that maintained them. We did occasionally borrow, a pilot to 'Air Test' the Lancs as their mods etc. were checked out and were ready for delivery, Some of my contemporaries did get the odd 'flip' with the borrowed pilot but somehow I always had something to do, so I never got a 'flip' in this delightful aircraft, much to my annoyance. Now I suppose I never will. I did quite a few hours in the Stirling, most at night when borrowing other folk's runways, while their crews were away upsetting Hitler, sometimes acting as supernumerary flight engineer.

I did enjoy my day at Waterbeach, the very moving service in the lovely old church, having lunch in the NCOs Mess. The run round the airfield in the bus. Tearing down No.1 runway at 55 mph, with not a flicker of 'Lift Off' in spite of everyone leaning forward. I had a quiet walk around on my own, loved the thousand trees that have now been planted all beginning to mature and looking very lush. Noted, where the ATC used to camp under canvas during their week with us in the summer time, getting the odd flight in a Tiger Moth and latterly an Airspeed Oxford. Everywhere very quiet, no sound of a Merlin or Hercules bellowing to get such a heavy load off the ground.

Bernard Yeomans

Former LAC Fitter IIE, 1537455 Bomber Command,

Member RAFA, Stirling Aircraft Assoc.

In a second letter Bernard tells of his encounter at Waterbeach, with the artist Dame Laura Knight and her painting entitled 'TAKE OFF'. On arriving at his regular charge Stirling 'S' Sugar to do a D.I. he found this 'dear lady' firmly ensconced, just where the flight engineer is in the painting, facing the cockpit. Having been brought up on a diet of Nazi Paratroopers disguised as nuns, he reported his findings to a much harassed Chiefie Welch who reassured him that she was a distinguished 'Artist' and an R.A. to boot and not to be molested or annoyed in anyway. So a young and very green airman was privileged to see a great artist at work making her preliminary pencil sketches. Bernard has kindly enclosed a copy of this painting, the original of which measures 72" x 60" and can be seen in the Imperial War Museum.

Harry Gilmore, Wireless Operator

(Pilot : John Topham)

On the 3rd of August 1944 we were briefed to carry out one of the many daylight raids that were going on at that time (after D Day) on Northern France. These raids were shorter compared to the night raids on Germany which we had carried out in the winter of the early part of the year. This raid on the 3rd August 1944 was our 27th trip and we were as a crew, I believe, feeling rather good and optimistic of finishing our tour of 30 bombing trips. However this was not to be.

As I recall, we had reached the target without any undue trouble, and had just dropped our bombs and leaving the target area when things happened very quickly. There were sudden shouts of "We're going down - a bomb's gone through our wing". I clearly remember going down with the aircraft for what must have been of course only seconds, when I seemed to remember 'John' our pilot shouting "Hold on". Obviously he must have managed to regain control of the aircraft, for we were next coming down to crash land close to some woods.

Our pilot obviously crash landed our Lancaster very well, for we all survived the crash, and managed to get out of the aircraft quickly. However the pilot broke his leg in the crash, and had to be left at a farmhouse. Three of the crew, Flight Engineer, Mid Upper Gunner, and myself - the Wireless Operator, were picked up in a wood by German troops within minutes, ending up prisoners of war. However the Bomb Aimer and Navigator who were with the Pilot at the farmhouse managed to get to Paris, only to be picked up five days later, also ending up prisoners of war.

Three days after we crashed, that same area including the farmhouse was over-run by our troops having pushed back the German troops. As a result our Pilot was eventually flown back to England.

I must say that I was always aware of the possibility of being 'shot down', but never being 'bombed down' by one of our own aircraft.

NOTE: Coincidentally, a photocopy of a newspaper cutting, from The London Daily Mail, dated sometime in 1949, has kindly been presented by Fred Brown (ex 514 M.U.G. but not of this crew) from Australia. Fred says, "John Topham was a huge man, always knew when he was about".

The cutting states: John Topham, D.F.C. was piloting a Lancaster Bomber over France one day in 1944. A bomb from another plane hit his and he had to crash land. French people hid him by 'burying' him in a grave. They gave him air pipes to breathe through. Germans hunted for the bomber crew, and the Frenchmen showed them the grave. So the Germans saluted respectfully, and left. Later, Topham, D.F.C., was "exhumed". He made his way back to England. When the war was over he joined Newcastle Police.

Thomas H. Harvell, Flight Engineer

Tom Harvell

Pilot F / O Robert Jones
Navigator F / Sgt George Robertson
B / Aimer F/ O Kenneth Loader
W / Op F / Sgt Frank Jones
F / E Sgt Thomas Harvell
M / U Gunner Sgt Robert Lane
R / Gunner Sgt Alfred Braine

Tom Harvell tells his remarkable story

As a 19 year old 'sprog' Flight Engineer, I joined 1678 Conversion Flight, Waterbeach, in April 1944. There I crewed up with pilot Robert (Bob) Jones, aged 22, and crew. The only street-wise member of the crew was Robby the navigator who had done some op's on 'Wimpies' in North Africa. We became a very close knit crew on and off flying. All N.C.O.'s were accommodated in a Nissen hut. The crew joined the Squadron at the end of May and our pilot showed his skills a week later in saving us from disaster during an op' on Valenciennes when he evaded a rocket firing aircraft in a series of corkscrews. Several op's that followed all against V1 sites, Pas de Calais area, were fairly non eventful.

Then came a daylight raid on the 30th June against Panzers poised at Villers Bocage, Normandy, for a night offensive against Monty's troops, that received the grateful thanks of Monty to all concerned (through Bomber Harris).

Three New Zealand crew members shared our Nissen hut. On one op' their Lanc did not return and we had the morbid sight of their kit being packed up and being taken away.

On the 17th July we were given a break from the Squadron. We had just been allocated a brand new Lanc III, when we were sent with it to RAF Rowley Mile at Newmarket. There, equipment relating to the new GH was installed and we spent the next five days flying with boffins on board on tests over Wales. When the tests were completed we returned to the Squadron leaving behind our flying test bed Lanc and then did our first op over Germany proper, to Kiel, followed by a gruelling 7½ hour op' to Stuttgart the next night.

Two nights later on 28/29 July we went back to Stuttgart but never arrived. At about 01.30 hours over eastern France, which was still occupied by the Germans, we flew out of cloud into brilliant moonlight. Alf, the rear gunner, reported lighter flares and the next moment two bursts of cannon fire struck us. The port inner engine caught fire and our Lanc started to go down. An explosion blew me out through the bomb aimers' observation window. I steered my parachute sideways to avoid burning debris. This took me away from the crash area of the burning wreckage of our Lanc, but the only other survivor, Robby the navigator, fell near it and was taken prisoner.

After hiding my parachute and Mae West (found by the Germans next day) I came across a male nurse on a road - who was cycling home from the hospital in the town of Neufchateau, to his home in the village of Brancourt. There he tended my head wounds and hid me in the loft of his house. There was a hunt for me, but alter live days my French friend gave me an old suit of his and with a friend of his all three of us cycled to the cemetery at Neufchateau, where my fellow crew members who had not made it were buried in a communal grave. I walked past a scruffy German soldier on duty at the cemetery gates to find the grave was covered in a mountain of flowers still being added to. I spent the night in a safe house at Neufchateau and was taken by a charcoal driven car to a countryside mill next day. There I met up with a French Canadian, Sgt rear gunner, sole survivor of a Stirling that had crashed on a supply dropping mission to the 'Resistance'. His name was Paul Bell.

We travelled on together with the aim of crossing into Switzerland, but upon reaching the mountains at the border in the Tranche Comte, we decided to stay and fight with the Resistance guerrilla arm - the Marquis. I joined as a Marquisard under the name of Charles Hautier and was issued with identity papers under that name. I was issued with a revolver, with ammo and a tri-coloured armband bearing the cross of Lorraine.

The local German army Commandant, frustrated by our rail sabotage and truck ambushes, called in a 400 strong battalion of Ukrainian SS troops from Alsace to wipe us out. However contact was made with senior N.C.O's and as a result the whole battalion deserted to our mountain strongholds and our combined forces then liberated the region ahead of the arrival of U.S. 7th Army and French 1st Army forces from the south. Paul Bell and I were probably the only RAF personnel who fought alongside German Army troops without being traitors.

Paul and I then hitch hiked down to Naples, Italy, by U.S. Airforce planes where we contacted the RAF who held us in custody until our identities were established. We were flown back to the UK where we were debriefed and sent on leave. It was then November and we were told that our operational days were over in the European theatre of war as we had breached rules of the Geneva Convention through our clandestine activities in France.

111

I did however during my leave make a one day visit to the Squadron giving the Engineer Leader the surprise of his life. From leave I was sent to RAF Cosford to take a course of new category of aircrew - 'Aircrew Leader', when I was then posted to 1665 Conversion Unit at Woolfox Lodge in this capacity.

In the winter of 1945 I was posted again to Waterbeach as Aircrew Leader but the mighty Lancs had gone having been replaced by Transport Command Liberators. Paul Bell sadly, although taken off operational flying, was killed when flying as a gunnery instructor in a Stirling that crashed.

To end on a technical note, I would mention that when on the Squadron I crewed all three marks of the Lanc. My preference was for the Mark II.

Tom further adds:

A few years ago, the Imperial War Museum recorded approximately two hours of audio tapes on a wider scale relating to those experiences and the tapes have been placed in the archives of the museum for posterity.

Part of our stricken Lancaster (LM 206) lives on. A port Merlin engine was salvaged in remarkably good condition, being recovered from the bed of the river Meuse 50 years after the event. It has been refurbished by the French Air Force and is now exhibited in the base museum of the 'top gun' air base at St Dizier, Eastern France.

My five fellow crew members who were killed still rest in the cemetery in the town of Neufchateau now in separate graves. I have a daughter living in Eastern France so I visit the graves from time to time. No crew photos are available, my skipper was superstitious about photos.

Tom Harvell Flight Engineer, whose fascinating story appears earlier, has written again describing his recent meeting with the night tighter pilot who

Luftwaffe photograph of Hauptmann Heinz Rökker, whose 63 night victories included at least two aircraft from 514 Sqn.

shot him and his crew mates down. Many will find the following account disturbingly thoughtful.

Further to my previous 514 Squadron experiences relating to being shot down by a night fighter on the 28 / 29th July, 1944, over Neufchateau, Eastern (occupied) France, with the loss of 5 fellow crew members.

On the 10th September last year (1999) at Neufchateau, I had the unique experience of meeting the night fighter pilot of the Junkers 88 who shot down our Lanc. He is 83 year old Heinz Rökker, ex highly decorated air ace with 64 kills to his credit. He spoke English well and we relived that fateful night which he clearly remembers. He had been traced by a friend of mine who is

113

in the aviation business in Germany and who was able to gain access to Luftwaffe wartime records.

Heinz told me the following that goes a long way to explain Bomber Command's high losses.

Most of his many 'kills' were carried out using 'Shräge Musik' (slanting music), the upward firing guns fitted to the top of the fuselage of his Junker's 88. Attacking unseen, from the blind spot beneath a bomber, he was rarely fired at by gunners and not once in his 64 combats was his fighter hit by return fire. In regard to the 'corkscrew' manoeuvre, he said that he did not follow a bomber into this manoeuvre but just slackened speed and maintained his heading. Invariably the bomber would surface ahead of him in his sights and as it did so it would be despatched by his nose cannons. He stated that he was grateful for H2S and MONICA that gave off signals that allowed his radar operator to home in quite easily on a bomber.

I suppose, all in all, it feels better to have been shot down by a highly skilled night fighter ace than some novice pilot. We paid homage to my crew members buried in the town cemetery and attended a civic reception hosted by the Mayor who looked on the meeting as a reconciliation of former enemies and their respective homelands.

Tom added that Heinz Rökker is a retired University Professor and a very nice chap, and that he hopes to see him again at his home near Bremen. Tom has read the account of the death of flight engineer Harry Osborn, finding it profound and to which he adds:

I have no doubt now that his Lanc was the bomber I saw in blazing outline on open ground on the Pas de Calais just before an unsuccessful attack by a night-fighter on us when we were returning from Valenciennes. I have always thought that the bomber must have made a crashed landing in flames as opposed to plunging in. The letter written by sole survivor, Aussie Navigator Arnold Morrison, seems to indicate that this was the case.

Robert C. Chester – Master, Rear Gunner

Flt. Sgt. Bob Chester-Master, Rear Gunner, was one of three Australians in a crew which arrived at the Squadron in July 1944, their pilot, Flt. Sgt. John Lawrie, being from New Zealand. Their 13th operation on the night of 12/13th August (not good omens for the superstitious) proved to be unlucky. The following extracts from Bob's story describe some of the events that began for him on that night.

The morning of the 12th.August 1944 dawned clear. Having flown five missions in the last seven days and nights, now it should be our turn to have a break. Our joy was to be short lived. On reporting to our flight headquarters, we found that we were listed for that night. Although we would not be taking off until 2000 hours, there was much to prepare for the night's mission. Briefing on the weather was first. We could expect cloud of varying thickness on the way to, over target and on the way home. Not a lot of cloud cover to help protect us, but we had to accept small mercies. The various section heads went through their spiel and then it was time for the target to be revealed. RUSSELSHEIM, a town in the south west of Germany, where the local Opel factory was making wings for the V1 (buzz bomb), which was wreaking havoc in London and the surrounding areas. Our job was to 'knock it out' of production.

Each aircraft would be loaded with 13000 lbs of high explosive bombs, plus canisters of fire bombs. A total of 297 aircraft would participate, comprising 191 Lancasters, 96 Halifaxes and 10 Mosquitoes. The ground crew were making their final checks. A few brief moments of banter, good luck, safe return wishes and now it was our turn. Each man climbed into the plane to take up their positions, as I crawled to the rear. Before opening the turret doors, it was necessary for me to stow my parachute in the rack on the port side of the fuselage, as there was no room inside the turret. In my bulky outfit, I settled in and carried out my preflight checks. Turret rotation, depressing and elevating the guns, checking mechanisms and searching for oil leaks from the firing rams. With a check of the reflector sights and a final wipe of the inside of the perspex, which was my only protection from the elements, I was ready for whatever the night would bring.

One by one, the crew reported all systems go and we were ready for takeoff. The four throttles were gradually opened and we were on our way to the main runway. We were number three for takeoff, 30 secs behind number two. The green light shone steady and we were on our way to the night's adventure. Gradually speed increased -ninety-five, one hundred, one hundred and five as the tail lifted. (I was always first off and last down). The skipper lifted from the runway and started the climb. The wheels folded away and we became a clean dark and brutal shadow, loaded with fuel, fire and explosive.

We had joined the stream at 7000 feet and began the slow climb to operational height. At 10000 feet, all crew connected to oxygen, to prevent altitude sickness and unconsciousness. I turned on my heating system and gradually felt the warmth flowing through, but as we climbed higher, it would be barely sufficient. Our track would take us across the enemy coast in a south easterly direction, thus avoiding the heavier anti-aircraft fire along the Dutch coast. We also knew that the German defences would now be alerted to our coming and it would only be a matter of time before we met the opposition. The Germans had very sophisticated radar and could quickly alert all anti-aircraft batteries, as well as the Luftwaffe, who, in this area, were using JU88's with very heavy fire power - 7.62mm machine guns and up to five 20mm cannon. Ahead, the horizon was brightening and tonight the moon would arise to near full and we realised that this would help the enemy fighters when it came time to turn homewards.

As we left the target area under the orange lit cloud of smoke and dust, I could not help but wonder what carnage we had caused. Time over target had been 0015 hours, which meant a very high state of concentration for 4 hours and we still had a long way to get home. The eyes were getting very tired and it was becoming difficult to focus as there was only the framework of the turret and the guns and the darkness.

Suddenly, the night sky was aglow with green tracer bullets snaking towards us - we were under attack. Quickly ordering "corkscrew starboard ~ go", I opened fire at the dark object at about 300 yards - it was the dreaded JU88 night fighter. He had come from below and as he came closer and then broke away to port, he gave me a wonderful opportunity to rake his fuselage. A fire started and even in the darkness I could see pieces breaking off his plane. He then rolled over and went into a dive, trailing smoke and fire. He was mortally wounded - a victory to us (later confirmed).

The mid-upper gunner came on the intercom to report - "Skipper, starboard inner hit - it's on fire". The engineer reached for the graviners to work the fire extinguishers - "Engine feathered, skipper". The mid-upper gunner now reported that he could see fuel flowing over the port wing, but a check of the panels, indicated it was more likely to be engine coolant, so the port outer was also shut down. The skipper reported loss of control of the aircraft and ordered "Bale out, bale out, we are down to 2000 feet". This did not give us much time, as I still had to centre my turret, open the doors, crawl out and take my parachute from its storage rack. Ripping off my gloves, I fumbled with the clips as I crawled to the rear door.

Up front, the skipper was trying to hold the plane level, as the engineer, bomb aimer and navigator, dropped through the hatch. By doing this, he did not have time himself and as I found out much later - went down with his plane. Meanwhile we kept losing height and I could see the rear escape door open and realised that I was the last to leave from this exit. Reaching the door, I could see the ground below and flung myself into the night. It was theoretic practice to count to seven before pulling the ripcord, but there was no time for that and I pulled as I jumped. I felt the parachute open, but almost immediately hit the ground very heavily and felt a surge of pain shoot up my left foot. I estimate that I had jumped from about 700 feet and that the 'chute had not fully opened. The pain in my leg now became intense, so I opened my escape 'kit' and swallowed a couple of pain killers. As soon as some of the pain was relieved, I crawled to the nearest haystack and burrowed into the base, where I fell into an exhausted sleep.

Daylight was streaming through the hay when I awoke - less exhausted, but the pain from my foot was intense and sending shafts up the leg. Thoughts now raced through my mind - was I the only survivor or had some or all of the crew made it? This question was not to be answered until much later. The major question of the moment was what to do now. Here I was, a 19 year old Australian flyer, in a foreign country, thought to be Belgium, with absolutely no knowledge of the language, with what could be a broken leg, cold, hungry, thirsty and hundreds of miles behind enemy lines. A feeling of deep apprehension came over me and I felt a surge of self pity. Realising that this would not help the situation and that I would have to adopt a more positive attitude, I opened my escape kit, took out the silk map and spread it on the ground. These kits were carried on every trip and contained - pain killers, benzedrine, fishing line, chewing gum, chocolate, money of the countries over which we flew, water purifying tablets and the large silk map of the countries and one or two more items of which the memory fails.

The first thing really was to try and guess approximately where I might be and then take action to get away. Loosening my tie, I removed the collar stud and scratched off the paint to reveal a compass which had swung round to magnetic North. We also carried another hidden compass in the form of two buttons on the fly of our trousers. One button had a very fine needle inserted and the other was placed on top, so that a dot swung to magnetic North. They were to prove invaluable for aircrew to help them on their way.

I had not removed my boots and therefore was still not sure what had happened to my leg, but I resolved to get moving, in the hope that I might be able find a large stick to assist my movements. I removed my flying gear and with the parachute and Mae West, buried them deep in the haystack. I had spotted some woods in the distance and was about to start on my way when I saw a man with a dog walking across the field. The dog saw me and came bounding and barking. This activity drew the attention of the man who seemed hesitant as he followed. A very difficult attempt at conversation - he did not speak any English and I did not speak French or Flemish, but I gathered that he wanted to tell the Germans who could possibly help me with my leg. This idea did not sit too well with me and it seemed I had convinced him as he pointed to the woods and indicated that I should get there and hide and wait - but for what? Would it be help or danger? Obviously I had no option and I crawled and stumbled over and into the woods and sat down exhausted. I guessed the time to be about noon - my watch having been torn from my wrist during the hasty exit from the plane.

I was now even more thirsty and hungry, but decided against using the emergency rations at the moment. Evening drew on and I made a bed in the bracken, but spent a restless night, thinking that every sound was made by Germans looking for any surviving crew. I kept my trusty revolver close by in case of emergency. My leg was still giving me a lot of pain. Morning came and I heard a long but low whistle from the clearing but wait for some time before I crawl out to investigate. I found that an 'angel' had left food and water so I felt that I was not alone and maybe help would be forthcoming., but at least I was safe for the moment. The day dragged by - evening came, another whistle and more food.

On the third day, I heard crashing noises through the trees and held my revolver towards the area. Two men burst through the undergrowth and I realised they were of a friendly disposition and they indicated that they would return.

The next morning the men returned and the larger one lifted me on his back and I was on my way to whatever. After about twenty minutes we broke through into a clearing where I could see three pushbikes and I realised that I would have to ride one, but how could I with a bung leg. However, one was a fixed wheel and after being placed on the seat, my left foot was strapped to the pedal. The ride proved to be a very long one, away from the main roads and through the country lanes. We eventually arrived at a small village, where my boots were removed and an inspection of my leg was carried out. It was determined that I had fractured a bone in the ankle, so it was heavily strapped. Breakfast followed and then we were on our way again.

Another long ride to a safe house. Later I ascertained this was the home of Hector and Marie De Smet in the village of St.Lievens Houtem, South West of Brussels. This was to be my hideout for the time being. At least, I had shelter, food and a reasonable degree of safety thanks to my helpers, one of whom was Norbert Van Herrewegh, and it was not until 48 years later in July 1992, that we met again.

Neither Hector nor Marie spoke any English but by persevering with sign language, I understood they wanted me to take off my uniform ready for a good scrub. They heated water on the stove and prepared an old tin tub for a good soak. As I slid into the water, it felt so good after days of wishing for one. I now felt a little easier in mind, having a roof over my head and in the hands of friends. After the luxury of the bath, Hector gave me some underwear, shirt and trousers to wear. My uniform was taken, never to be seen by me again. My ankle, still painful, was strapped as it was indicated that I climb a ladder into the loft where a bed of straw had been prepared and I settled down in deep sleep.

Bob's story revealed many more fascinating experiences. Briefly, he was moved to a safe house in Brussels where he met up with his bomb aimer. An attempt was made to take them through the 'Comete' escape line to Spain but they had to return as the line had been broken further down and it was too dangerous to proceed. Similarly they had to return from an attempt to reach Switzerland. When Brussels was eventually liberated by the British Army they met up again with their navigator and on repatriation to England met up once again with the other three surviving crew members who had evaded capture in Belgium. Of these, the wireless operator, George Durland, had broken a leg on landing and was taken prisoner, but later escaped from the train taking him to Germany.

Lancasters at Waterbeach

Bob has returned a number of times in later life to meet his Belgian helpers, now his friends, and cannot praise too highly their courage in risking death and torture in assisting our airmen.

CREW: Pilot Flt. Sgt John Lawrie, RNZAF

F / E Flt. Sgt Tom Young RAF

B /A Flt. Sgt. Martin Carter RAF

W/Op Sgt George Durland RAF

Nav Flt. Sgt Reg Orth RAAF

M / U/ G Flt. Sgt Sam Burford RAAF

R/ G Flt. Sgt Robert Chester-Master RAAF

Corb Stewart, Air Bomber

Corb Stewart - RCAF, commenced his service life in Toronto in September 1942 and qualified as Air Bomber in October '43 before coming to England for further training. He said that crewing up at O.T.U. in March '44 was a momentous event:

After supper, got together and crewed up, seem like a good bunch of guys. I say momentous as we were to eat, sleep, fly, bitch and travel together until December '44. Crewing-up was not done on any scientific basis, instead the various trades - pilots, navigators, bomb aimers, wireless ops and air gunners were allowed to mingle together and if you met someone compatible you would ask "Would you like to crew up" (sort of like getting married). As I hazily recall Al Violet (navigator) and myself took a shine to each other and were shortly joined by Frank, Don, Jim and John - a crew of six. The flight engineer, George, joined the crew when we started training on four engine bombers.

This crew arrived at Waterbeach early August `44. Frank flew his 'second dicky' trip shortly afterwards, during which the rear gunner shot down a FW19O. Their tour of operations included four attacks on Homberg and two on Essen, their last target being Neuss on the night of 28/ 29th November. Although frequently damaged by flak they all came through unscathed.

Crew:

Frank Heald Pilot age 24
Alan Violet Nav 19
Corb Stewart Air / B 22
Les Baldwin W/Op 20
George Cuthbertson F /E 20
Jim Turner M/U/G 19
John Shaughnessy R/ G 19

Hugh C Richford, Pilot

Pilot Hugh 'Richie' Richford at the controls on a daylight attack near the target, Siegen, 16th December 1944.

F/ Sgt Richford ('Richie' to his crew) with his all NCO crew arrived at Waterbeach early in August 1944. He would successfully complete his tour as Flying Officer, with DFC to follow, and here relates some of his experiences:

For the final seven months of the war, the squadrons of 3 Group were equipped with the blind bombing aid GH. This enabled the group to operate independently on many days of that winter when the continent was cloud covered. In retrospect, the accuracy of GH proved to have made a worthwhile contribution to the offensive, especially against oil targets.

The bombing was carried out by aircraft flying in 'vics' of three, the leader having the GH equipment and the crew trained to operate it. The other two crews merely had to hold formation, open bomb doors when the leader opened his, and release their bombs the moment the leader's bombs were seen to start falling. If one were not a leader there was a feeling that the full abilities of the crew were not being utilised particularly in the skills of bomb aiming and navigation. Also, there was little to be seen apart from bombs falling into

Vic of three 514 Squadron aircraft on a GH daylight attack, December 1944, viewed from the Flight Engineer's position. Lancaster A2-G, PA186, was probably being flown at the time by F/L Ron Pickler, RCAF, DFC.

Press photograph on the occasion of the final operation for F/O Richie Richford and crew (to Trier on 21ˢᵗ December 1944). The two women were Mlle H Edouard and Mlle H Carion, members of the French Resistance who had assisted shot-down airmen. Crew L to R: Sgt Denis Ratcliffe (MU gunner); Sgt Harry Dison, flight engineer; F/S Geoff Norris, wireless operator; F/O Bill Ledingham, navigator; P/O Ernie Emmett, bomb aimer; Sgt Wally Morrison, rear gunner; F/O Richie Richford, pilot (Harry Dison).

cloud; none of the spectacle of night attacks or of some visual day targets which remain imprinted on the memory.

There were, of course, varying amounts of flak though sometimes none. It could be worrying particularly if one were in the leading vic and not protected by 'window', a situation which, on one occasion, resulted in an 88mm shell passing through our port wing without exploding. The other worry was other people's bombs, made more acute by the accuracy of GH concentrating everyone at the same release point.

Gunners: Wally and Rats.

In common with other crews who were well advanced in their tour, we were not given training as GH leaders. Apart from odd incidents and having to get out of bed in the small hours of cold mornings, only two of our GH trips stand out in the memory - the first and the penultimate.

The first was on the last day of August 1944 and was our seventh op. It was at least six weeks before the GH attacks got properly under way. It must have been a trial run by the Squadron. Who the leaders were or what training they had had I do not know. I doubt if I had heard of GH before the briefing. Martin Middlebrook's *Bomber Command War Diaries* note that eight targets were attacked that day, all believed to be 'V' weapon supply dumps. Our target was Pont Remy, near Abbeville, which was stated to be defended by four heavy guns. We were allotted A2 F, a new paddle bladed Mk 1 Lanc, the first replacement for the old Mk IIs of C Flight. As might be expected it was the Flight Commander's aircraft. He was at pains to tell me to take great care of it; I did not like to

125

remind him that we had flown it to Stettin and back two nights before without a blemish.

We were at No 3 (port aircraft) in the vic and I closed up as we ran into the target at 15,000 feet on that clear summer evening. Just before we got there something went wrong with the GH run and round we went for another attempt. We bombed, but by then we were the only three aircraft around and the four guns of Abbeville, which had not previously been in evidence, decided to shoot. The shells burst just off our port wing and close enough to be heard above the noise of four Merlins and through the thickness of a flying helmet. A quick check produced rather breathless replies, but all was well and there was no vital damage. The rear gunner kept a wary eye on a hole in the starboard elevator, which enlarged slowly in the slipstream as we journeyed home but we landed without incident.

Back at dispersal, the C.O. and an unhappy looking Flight Commander were inspecting the damage before I had climbed out. A thin stream of fuel was dribbling from the port wing, there were some twenty five to thirty holes down the port side of the fuselage and the elevator hole was large enough to stand up in. The rear gunner showed us his flying boot torn by a splinter and the mid-upper marvelled that he had been facing starboard and the back of his turret had taken the blast. It was a salutary lesson that going round again could be a threat to one's health and we avoided doing so until our penultimate operation.

On the 15th December we took off into the murk to attack the railway yards at Siegen, a little bombed target east of Cologne. We joined up with our leader and No 2 without much trouble but before reaching the south coast we were recalled; our England based fighter escort was grounded by the weather. We added a few bombs to the jettison area off Eastbourne.

The next day we tried again. The weather was even murkier but we were told that American Lightnings would be able to get airborne from their continental base to escort us. We climbed into a warm front. We were in cloud at the rendezvous height for our formation. Then up to the alternative height and, still in cloud, it was time to set our course out of touch with the others. We carried on climbing becoming well frosted on the outside. Then all four engines began to surge disconcertingly with the less common carburettor icing, quickly identified by the engineer and rectified with 'hot air'.

We were well over the continent by the time we broke horizontally out of the wall of cloud, soon followed by a gaggle of Lancasters. There was no chance of finding our own leader but, by that time in the GH story, such a contingency had been catered for by painting yellow stripes on the tail fins of all leader aircraft. A leader could then be sorted out and followed to the bomb release point. A good idea but, unfortunately, all aircraft with yellow markings were not always flown by GH qualified crews. This applied to us that day flying our own pet Lanc A2 Easy. Worse still, we were ahead of all the others and almost immediately the gunners were reporting other aircraft seeking to formate on us. For an awful minute or two we were leading some hundred aircraft to a target, obscured by a cloud layer below, with no means of aiming the bombs.

In those days of R/T silence there was no easy way of warning others not to follow us. All I could do was to waggle the wings, tell the wireless op to fire a red Very, and turn steeply to port hoping that no one would follow. Looking round I saw a few Lancs turn to follow us but I also saw, thankfully, that some stalwart was pressing on in the lead.

We came out of a 360° turn at the rear end of the stream and I sought some leader to formate on with great urgency, knowing we must be close to the target. The seconds ticked by. Suddenly there was a Lanc a bit above us to starboard with its bomb doors open. There followed moments of confusion. I yelled to the bomb aimer that this was the leader to bomb on, opened the bomb doors and pulled up to formate on him. The bomb aimer and others who could see outside knew better than I but I had given them no time to speak. Another moment and I too knew what was wrong - the other aircraft closed its bomb doors. We had overflown the target without bombing.

There was nothing else for it; once more it was round again. I turned quickly to port on to the reciprocal course. There had been some flak on the way in (two squadron aircraft were damaged) but fortunately there now appeared to be none over the target. There were some groans of disapproval over the intercom; after all it was our 29th op and the poor gunners could see the rest of the stream rapidly disappearing in the distance. After what seemed an age, but no doubt far too soon for accuracy, I turned in and we hurriedly bombed on the green sky markers that the GH leaders always dropped.

The rest of the Lancs were but dots miles ahead and there was no sign of the escort, though they may well have been keeping an eye on us. Boost and revs were quickly pushed up to plus seven, twenty-six fifty, and we went roaring after the others. It was not long before a lone Lanc came into view, a bit below and to starboard. It had one engine feathered. I lost sight of it as it fell behind. We had not reached the tail end of the main stream but I felt we could slow down a bit and reduced power. As I did so, the urgent voice of the rear gunner was warning that the lone Lanc behind had been attacked by fighters and was on fire. Suddenly out to port were two Lightnings and two Me.109's locked in tight turns just above the cloud tops. I looked back into the cockpit to push up the power again and seconds later looked back for the fighters. Just as suddenly they had disappeared.

We soon caught up with the others and were back in the frontal cloud again, heading for home with kind thoughts for our US escort. Records show that the Lanc shot down came from IIS Squadron, 'up the road' at Witchford. Sadly only three of the crew survived.

Earlier on this same day, 16th December, the bad weather had covered the start of the German offensive in the Ardennes. It was not until 21st Dec., and after several cancellations, that it cleared sufficiently for us to attack the marshalling yards at Trier, behind the battle. It was an uneventful trip and, as a crew, we had dropped our last bombs.

CREW: Pilot F/ O Hugh Richford age 21
(Ranks end of tour) Nav Sgt Dix 23 (Pont Remy)
F / O Bill Ledingham 21 (Siegen)
B / A P /O Ernie Emmett 21 RCAF
W / Op F / Sgt Geof Norris 23
F / E Sgt Harry Dison 19
M/ U Sgt Denis Ratcliffe 19
R / G Sgt Wally Morrison 21

John Jeffries, Bomb Aimer

John volunteered for the RAFVR when still at school. A travelling Board', consisting of one Wing Commander, had a chat with him in the head's study and told him that subject to medicals he was accepted for training as a pilot. When John entered service the PNB system had started and he qualified as a bomb aimer.

Having passed through various courses including training in Canada, he was at 84 O.T U Desborough in the summer of 1944.

The crew was:
Tom Marks, Pilot
Bill Harradine, Nav
John Jeffries, B/A
Bob Jenkins W / Op (RAAF)
Tom Evans, M/U/G
Bill Hough, R / G
Paddy Mills, F /E

John states:

One incident at OTU was always remembered although it could have been more serious. We were doing dinghy drill in a hangar, when a yell came from Tom Marks, who, in his hurry to get into the dinghy had fallen from the cockpit to the ground. Fortunately he only suffered a broken leg. However, something we always remembered was when he came round, he said "I never did like b ...... y Wellingtons". He had completed his first tour in the Middle East on them.

His spell in hospital held up our training and so we left Desborough after the rest of the course. All the W /Ops on our course were in the RAAF and they were a great bunch of chaps. We then proceeded to Chedburgh where we picked up Paddy Mills our F/E, and thence to Feltwell. We eagerly awaited

Back row, left to right: John Jeffries, Bill Harradine, Tom Marks, Bob Jenkins.
Front row: Tom Evans, Bill Hough. Photo taken at 84 OUT, Desborough.

our posting to a Squadron and I recall Tom Marks telling us it was 514, with the remark "Gen crews to gen Squadrons".

We arrived by the usual open truck at Waterbeach in mid-September 1944. We did our first op' to Neuss on 23 Sept '44 and our last as a crew on 27th November. The next day Tom Marks was taken off ops as he was on his second (shorter) tour. It was a great disappointment as we were a happy and well organised crew. We got on very well together and spent much of our leisure time going out in twos and threes either to Cambridge or to one of the 'locals'. During the operations we had very little unusual experiences and we managed to keep out of trouble. The aircraft was hit quite often but fortunately none of the crew suffered any injury. The remaining crew members expected to get another pilot to complete their tour, but in the event they flew as relief crew members. John flew with F/O Stan Wright whose B/A was in Ely Hospital, finishing his tour on 11 Jan '45, a daylight to Krefeld.

Some of the Story of 514 Squadron

Bob Jenkins, Wireless Operator/AG,

Bob, an Australian from Victoria, and crew mate of John Jeffries, was accepted for aircrew and placed on a waiting list for entry in 1941. When Japan entered the war all 18 and 19 year olds, including future aircrew, were grabbed by the army, in which he served for 10 months, before attaining transfer to the RAAF. The wireless course was at Parkes in New South Wales where he flew in old Wacketts with pilots he was none too happy with. Then to Port Pirie for gunnery with pilots in Fairy Battles who were inclined to loop the loop with three scared budding air gunners. Bob says that he nearly fell out on one loop. After graduating and final leave he embarked on the USS Watsonia from Brisbane for New Zealand and San Francisco. Pullman carriages took them to New York where they boarded the Queen Elizabeth with 17,000 Yanks and 500 RAAF and RAF for Scotland. After further postings and training he crewed up at O.T.U., all other crew members being RAF. Bob states: Our pilot Tom Marks (second tour) called us 'The Clots'- talked too much, all thumbs, always lost. Then to Desborough on Stirlings, and Paddy Mills our Engineer joined us. So we got to know each other and went to Lancaster Finishing School at Feltwell where we got to know the wonderful Lancaster. Finally to 514 Squadron at Waterbeach.

Tom, flying as '2nd dickie' on the first 'op' came back and never called us 'The Clots' again. He said that the Canadian crew were worse than us, talked, smoked, swore and scared him stiff. Our first operation was to Neuss in the Ruhr. It was so pretty - search lights, flickering flak, photo flashes, the odd violent and big flash as someone blew up - or were they 'scarecrows'? A few bumps and near misses, masses of flame and burning on the ground, rolling smoke. You could see the glow in the sky almost back to the coast.

And so we bashed the Ruhr, Essen, Cologne, Düsseldorf Gelsenkirchen, oil refineries at Homberg, Bottrop, Solingen and other places. Night ops and then a series of daylight operations in front of Monty's armies. On one trip we saw another Lancaster in trouble, two engines smoking. So Tom flew alongside from Homberg to Belgium to keep him company. It was from 514, the pilot John Tolley. We saw him land in a field, then came home, glad we had helped someone by our company. We were hit on most occasions, holes in the wings and bomb bay doors. On one trip, 10/10 cloud all the way, but sunny over the target - Bottrop I think - planes flying in all directions, someone dropped his load across three of our 514 Lancasters, blew up one and sent the other two sideways with the blast.

Our biggest fright was over Essen when we were hit badly. Tom Marks did a great job and got us home. When we came in to land, he discovered one of our wheels was damaged, so he landed on one wheel, jabbing the damaged wheel down every so often. We ground looped about three times before coming to a stop. The crash crew were excellent and pulled us out very smartly.

I had some wonderful leaves with my crew. John Jeffries, our bomb aimer, came from Fairly Wallop in Hampshire. Imagine as an Australian, I found Nether Wallop, Middle Wallop and Little Wallop. John's father was valet to Robert Wallop, the Earl of Portsmouth, I think. His stories, of people he served and met, enthralled me. John's parents became my English parents while I was over there. Bill Harradine, our navigator, took me to Hackney in London - what a city. Tom Evans took me to Manchester in summer. Told me to bring my great-coat, but I knew better - it was summer. I froze.

Finally Tom Marks departed and our crew split up. I crewed up with F/O John Tolley, pilot of the Lancaster we had escorted from Homberg to Belgium. Again I was lucky with my RAF pilots. They were good and a joy to fly with. John Tolley liked to sit under his Canadian pal's Lancaster and scare the daylight out of the rear gunner. With John Tolley most of our ops were daylight. I remembered a sunny winter day, no cloud, snow on the ground and Ludwigshaven the target, the river winding through the town, bomb bursts and rippling shock waves in the snow.

And so my tour of 38 trips finished. I palled up with Dick Sherwood, engineer with the Base Test Crew, and flew with them testing new Lancasters before handing them over to the Squadrons. Dick was a fisherman and took me fishing on the Cam river. I received my commission, was posted back to Brighton, then posted to Millom in Cumberland. I visited the Navy, the Victory at Portsmouth and said my goodbyes to the old crew and their families. They were great to me and on my return home I sent them food parcels for many years. In 1972 I came back and had a reunion with four great friends and their families. Since then Bill Harradine, Tom Evans and Dick Sherwood have died, so John and I are the survivors. We have corresponded for over fifty years.

Don Forwood, Navigator

Henry (Tich) Taylor, M/ U/ Gunner, has presented us with accounts written by his fellow crew member, Navigator Don Forwood RAAF, from which the following is extracted:

Walcheren. On 3rd Oct. 1944 this crew took part in the attack on the seaward polder dyke of Walcheren Island, just south of Westkapelle, in order to flood a number of low lying gun positions and to isolate others on higher ground. These guns were vital to the Germans guarding the Scheldt Estuary and the approaches to the port of Antwerp, which the Allies badly needed to supply their northern armies.

The attack took place in the afternoon just prior to a tidal peak. The dyke was 200 feet wide and had been built up from sand, gravel and clay, reinforced below water level with hand plaited mattresses of willow rods anchored by stakes and weighted down by rocks - the result of centuries of Dutch experience. Their bomb load included a 4000 pounder and a number of 1000 pound bombs, some of which were delayed action. The weather was clear over the target and the bomb aimer got a very good hit adding to the craters already filling with water. Turning for home they could see the craters gradually blending to form a channel through the dyke. Subsequent aircraft reported a good break-through, and 617 Squadron, following if necessary with 'tall boy' bombs to finish the job, was called off Sadly, in spite of leaflet and broadcast warnings in advance of the attack, there were needless losses among the Dutch civilians as the German commander had ordered everyone to stay put.

On one of their trips to the Ruhr during the next fortnight, they passed close enough to see the breach in the dyke. By that time it was about 100 yards wide. Later in the month, on 28th October, they attacked German gun positions near Flushing (Vlissingen) on the higher ground at the southern tip of the Island. German resistance ceased by 9th November, and fifteen days later the first Allied ships were unloading at Antwerp.

Friendly or Unfriendly Fire. On 19th Oct '44 they were briefed for a night attack on the marshalling yards at Stuttgart an important supply junction for the German southern armies. The outward route was the usual circuitous approach to keep the enemy guessing the destination. The return route was also indirect and they were instructed to loose height in a shallow dive to 6000ft on leaving the target, to give a speedy departure and to put night fighters off the scent. The return route was to pass between Nancy and Metz, described as inner artillery zones to be avoided at all costs.

The outward journey passed without incident apart from bumping about in slipstreams all the way. Don, as navigator, welcomed such conditions, knowing that they must be on track or at least in good company. The bombing went well except for the usual Ack Ack (flak) and the shallow dive down to 6000 ft. was very bumpy. The winds calculated at 20,000 ft. were of no use at 6000 ft. Don, unable to get a reliable fix as the H2S was not performing well, had to rely on the forecast winds. They finally reached a point where they should be over friendly territory, staying alert for fighters but without fear of flak. Don was looking forward to a drink of tea from the W/Operator's flask when, without warning, they were hit by a string of four Ack Ack shells, the third one bursting right under the tail. The aircraft was thrown into a steep dive, Don ending up against the roof clawing at anything to try and regain his seat. The skipper at first unable to pull out of the dive, gave the order to bale out, but then managed to pull the nose up with such force that some of the crew were thrown against the floor. The bomb aimer told them later that as they pulled out of the dive he had seen tree tops racing past below.

A port engine was on fire and in the semi-darkness the engineer feathered and doused the port outer engine. Almost as he did so, he realised his mistake and shut down the correct engine. The skipper would not restart the port outer engine, as its extinguisher was exhausted and therefore potentially unsafe. The gyro in the distant reading compass had toppled, the Elsan contents spilled, and the hydraulic oil lines of the mid-upper turret had been severed adding to the mess. 'Tich', the mid-upper gunner had been hit by shrapnel just above the knee. The wireless operator got him onto the couch and applied sulphur drug powder to the wound, bandaged it and gave him morphine to ease the pain. There were over 120 holes in the aircraft, including one near the tail as big as a soccer ball, and the tail had suffered damage. The aircraft flew badly as well as uneconomically with two engines out on one side giving a yaw of seven degrees. Unsure the fuel supply was intact, the skipper asked for a direct course home and took the risk of re-starting the port outer engine. It performed well, but they were the last one back by quite a margin.

'Tich' Taylor was in hospital for several months but happily regained the use of his leg, albeit with a slight limp. The rear gunner overstayed his six days 'survivors' leave, so two replacement gunners were needed to finish the tour. The new gunners were from a crew split up by a crash. Both had been burned about the hands and face but their morale was excellent and the crew felt lucky to have them aboard.

Don Forwood later checked his log using positive fixes and winds obtained after coming within Gee range, carefully back-plotting the track to where the action had taken place. It transpired that they had been about 12 miles off the intended track in the vicinity of Nancy. Don agonised over the thought that had he been more persistent with the uncooperative HZS screen he may have avoided the trouble. But he would never know. Nor with the fluidity of the front line would he ever know whether they were hit by 'friendly' or unfriendly fire.

Crew: Pilot F/O Don Parks
Navigator F/O Don Forwood RAAF
B/Aimer F/O Charles Pfaff
W/Op F/Sgt Kevin Warren RAAF
Flt/Eng Sgt Eric Clempson
M/U/G Sgt Henry (Tich) Taylor
R/ G Sgt Ron Clarke
Replacement M/U/G Sgt Douglas Bacon RCAF
Gunners R/G Sgt Cyril Marjoram

Accidental Bomb Explosion

On 29th December 1944 at 1030 hours Lancaster PD325 in C Flight, being fully bombed up, was completely destroyed by the explosion of its own bombs. 'Mel' Melluish, a Corporal Armourer, informs us that the bomb load detonated totalled 11,000 lbs, being made up of a 'cookie' (4000 lbs) and a mixture of 500 lb and 250 lb bombs. He suspects that the likely cause was one of the 250 pounders. These were old bombs that would have been declared unfit for use in peace time conditions, but someone in authority had the bright idea that they may as well drop them on the enemy. It seems that with age they could exude some of their explosive content which crystallised on the casing. Regulations stated that these crystals should be removed with hot soapy water and a wooden scraper, but under pressure of work there wasn't time to do the necessary. There were also problems with the Whitlock Carriers holding pairs of the 250 lb bombs, which may have been a causative factor.

'Mel' further relates:

On the previous day, Thursday 28th Dec 1944, the Squadron was engaged on daylight raids and the armament staff had been warned to go for early tea as a maximum effort was required for the next day, for a deadline of 9.30am. I was suffering from a severe case of dermatitis and consequently on light duty, which meant no handling of bombs or loading. I was doing a permanent duty crew and doing the job of NCO i/c the servicing crew. The armourers were being pushed to the limit, loading two loads per day plus the occasional load change plus the normal servicing and were working up to 20 hours per day.

My best mate, Cpl John Westgarth, was another ex-regular airman, an ex-brat, who on this day had asked me if I would swap jobs with him, as he had become engaged to a Waaf and they wished to go out to celebrate. I had some doubts and a funny feeling about it, but after all he was my pal and it seemed only fair to do him a favour. So he was free to seal his engagement that night and I carried on and did his bomb loading. We finished around 0800 hrs and after a late breakfast tried to get some sleep before being called out to reload the planes again after their short operation. Upon hearing the horrendous explosion we all rushed round on our bikes to the armament office to discover the cause.

Mel's friend who had swapped shifts with him was among the dead, his engagement not lasting a full day. The Waaf he was engaged to, named Lee and known by all her acquaintances as 'Dixie', was an MT Driver mostly employed on the aircrew transports.

Nine airmen were killed:

Cpl J Westgarth
LAC D G Bichard
LAC S Bolton
AC2 D V Brewer
LAC R Davies
LAC G G Hayden
AC1 H G Leach
LAC L Smales
LAC F C Watson
Four airmen were injured:
Cpl N R Garnham LAC R Roberts LAC L A Southway LAC P Thompson
One Lancaster destroyed (PD 325). Six Lancasters damaged (including: NG 141, PD 324, NG 118, LM 727) some of which would not fly again.

Ron Goulding, Bomb Aimer

Ron Goulding with the crew of F/L Jimmy Parnell. The Lancaster is ME364, JI-P and the seventeen raid markings on her nose suggest that this photograph was taken at the end of hostilities.

Pilot F/L Jimmy Parnell age 24
Navigator F/O Les Seawood 24
Bomb Aimer F/ O Ron Goulding 22
W/Op W/O Don Matson 22 (RAAF)
F/E F/Sgt Brian Prudden 19
M / U Gunner W/O Harry Griffiths 30+
Rear Gunner W/O Les Gurr 30+
This crew arrived at Waterbeach in October 1944. Ron relates:

The majority of our ops were daylight targets in 'Happy Valley' (Ruhr), mainly targeting oil refineries and transport (marshalling yards etc._). On the night of **November 6th** we attacked Koblenz and suffered some damage to two of the engines, losing height slowly, and eventually broke through the cloud only to find that we were heading for the Alps. It soon became apparent that none of the compasses or directional finders were working correctly. I got out the Astro Compass and sighted the Pole Star and managed to return to base relying entirely on the Astro Compass.

Our most dicey trip was to Homberg on **20th November** when just after dropping the bombs the a/c on our port side exploded (we were in the box with a Vic of three a/c in front of us). Our aircraft, S Sugar, flew through the explosion and we appeared to lose control for a time. Thinking that we were hell bound for earth, I tried to put on my parachute but the gee force prevented me from doing so. However the skipper managed to regain control after a struggle, only to discover a large hole in the nose of the bomb aimer's position. The front turret had pieces of the other a/c wrapped around it and both gunners were slightly injured. We regained height and formated on several other Lancs as there were German fighters around. I therefore stayed in the front turret and to my surprise found it was working. It was however bitterly cold. The slight injuries to both gunners were patched up and they resumed their duties. On nearing the English coast the skipper's windscreen started to give way and the engineer held a large board over the screen to prevent it caving in. The difficulty was on landing, so I lay in the nose and guided the skipper down (some pilot training obviously of some use). When we landed the aircraft was found to be extensively damaged and I understand it was a write-off

At the time of the accidental bomb detonation, in late December, I was in the H2S Office not all that far from the explosion which killed several ground crew. I was just about to put a shovel of coal into the stove, and the coal was scattered around the office.

As far as I can recall we only had one positive attack by a fighter on a night raid, in which we corkscrewed and lost contact. On a daylight raid on Heligoland, **April 18th '45,** while on the bombing run, a fighter which I believe was a twin engined ME262, made an attack. We only saw it as it dived past our Lanc (lucky escape!)

That incidentally was our last operation before the European war ended. During the last few weeks we dropped food to the Dutch, and after the war ended we were kept busy transporting ex P.O.W's back from France.

The only time we came across intruders was during training at O.T.U. at Wing. Twice there, while on the circuit, we were told to disperse and on both occasions witnessed a/c blowing up on the final approach (intruders responsible?)

Cambridge was our happy hunting ground, and as a crew we went en masse and usually drank together in one of the pubs. The 'Baron of Beef and 'The Red Lion' were two of our favourites. The three officers in our crew were accommodated in a converted Nissen hut a short walk away from the mess. It's a sobering thought that although the chop rate was not as heavy as some previous periods, on three occasions the effects of crews who had gone missing were cleared from our room.

Our tour was a fairly brief but momentous time during our service life. We were a few trips short of our tour when Germany surrendered. We were then due to join 617 Squadron to go out east. However when the Far East war ended only the skipper joined 617.

Tony Baxter, Navigator

Back row, left to right: John Goldthorpe, Ron Taylor, Andy Deighton, Ken Grives.
Front row: Ron McGowan, Ray Foreman, Tony Baxter.

Tony crewed up at Market Harborough, 14 OTU (Operational Training Unit) in May 1944. At this stage of the war the standard aircraft at OTU was the twin engined Wellington, generally known as the 'Wimpey'. Tony's recollected snippets:

14 OTU. How we came to crew up I have no idea. Leaflet dropping over Wilhelmshaven and Paris, airsick for the only time in my life, and that was on the ground after circuits and bumps. A Stirling pronged in front of us when we were coming in to land which caused a rapid change of plan. No crash landings though we did have an engine on fire and this made for an emergency landing.

514 Squadron. On Lancs we suffered the usual flak damage but only landed at Woodbridge (emergency landing airfield) once. We had no technical problems, though I became known as 'The Blip Chaser'.

Stuck in the mud once just before take-off; after which our Lanc JI-F became known as 'Finger`, with that replacing the sword on the Squadron's Crest!

'Line shooting' now; at Leipzig once, we were the only plane from the Squadron to hit the target and our air photo was put on the notice board. On our first 'op' to the Ruhr, when over the target I was not frightened but thought of Coventry. The last op' when we had to go round again and thinking "Oh no, this can't happen to us now" - this was near Cologne on January 28th 1945.

The end of tour 'tie cutting ceremony' in the Brewery Tap outside the main gates. Really we were very lucky and by this time we had been together eight months.

Far East. After 514 Sqn I went to 276 Transport Sqn in Burma   quite hair raising after bombing, with only two engines on a clapped out Dakota   terrible weather and masses of mountains, a navigators nightmare with no radio aids.

After the Jap war was over we donned white suits and flew V.I.Ps back to their places of work between Calculated and Hong Kong. These included Pandit Nehru, Elsie and Doris Waters, and our own (514) Air Cdr Hard.

Crew (at 514):
Skipper Ray Foreman age 21
Navigator Tony Baxter 21
W / Op Ron Taylor
B / Aimer Ron McGowan 22
F / Eng John Goldthorp
M/U/G Ken Grives 19
R / G Andy Deighton

Joan Harrington, WAAF

WAAF, Joan Harrington (nee Williams) of the Base Registry, RAF Waterbeach, tells us that during the Spring of 1944 a WAAF Officer asked for volunteers to assist in welcoming returning aircrews. Joan writes:

When crews were due back after a bombing operation, we were asked to be up at the Camp one hour before, to prepare coffee, rum, etc. My friend and I (in the same hut) volunteered, and the WAAF Officer always woke us up in good time. Off we would go on our bikes (transport if bad weather) up to the base. It was rewarding for us to greet the crews who were usually very exhausted and glad of their coffee and rum. We found it very sad when crews were reported missing.

After the War finished, we were asked if we would like to have a trip in the Lancaster. The 9th July 1945 was the day chosen. We were briefed, weather forecast etc., and equipped with a parachute. We flew out over RAF Woodbridge and then to the Continent and on to our journey over the Ruhr. This will be forever in my memory. After seeing the dreadful devastation I wondered how ever all the places could be restored.

I will always be grateful for the opportunity I had to fly in a Lancaster. The journey lasted five hours.

F/O Donald Beaton, DSO, Pilot

This pilot took part in an attack on Le Havre on 8th Sept '44 during which the aircraft was hit by flak and severely damaged. It crash landed at Tangmere in Sussex, the pilot and flight engineer being badly injured. P/O E Nye (later Nav Leader) standing in for the crew's navigator, who was away on a `48`, sustained minor injuries.

In due course Don Beaton recovered from his injuries and recommenced flying duties with the Squadron. On 9th May '45, the day after V.E. Day (Victory in Europe) he took part in Operation `Exodus', the evacuation of ex-Prisoners of War. In addition to the crew of 6, there were 24 army POWs, ranging from Private to Captain in various regiments, as well as a Lieutenant in the U.S.A.A.F`. The Lancaster had taken off early from Waterbeach and commenced the return flight from Juvincourt at 12.15 hours. A message was sent from the aircraft at 12.25 stating that it was making a forced landing. The aircraft was observed to go into a flat spin and crash to the ground near Roye Ami. All the crew and passengers lost their lives.

On investigation it was not possible to account for the necessity for a forced landing, nor to establish definitely the cause of the crash. The position of the passengers to the rear of the fuselage indicated that the aircraft may have been tail heavy, but whether their incorrect positions were assumed before or after difficulties arose when the aircraft became out of control, could not be determined.

W/O F D Say supplied the information and copies of records relating to the above tragic incident. Don Say, Nav / Bomb Aimer, DFC, flew his second tour on 514 Squadron as bomb aimer with Donald Beaton, and finished his tour on 5th Sept '44 immediately prior to the Le Havre operation on which Don Beaton and others were injured.

Peter G Dean, Pilot (RAAF)

CREW: Pilot F / O Peter Dean
Navigator P / O George Mills
B /Aimer F / Sgt William Elliot
W / Op F / Sgt Charles Kemp
F / E Sgt Basil Holiday
M / U / G F / Sgt Martin Golightly
R / G F / Sgt Roy Griffiths

This Australian pilot enlisted in the RAAF in October 1941 but had to wait for a vacancy for training until July '42. Various delays and postings followed and he graduated as pilot in August '43 having trained on Tigers and Ansons. He journeyed by sea from Melbourne to San Francisco, then on to New York where he boarded the Queen Elizabeth for Scotland. Then to Brighton and various flying units before crewing up at 26 OTU at Wing, in early July

'44. After some delay this crew went on to 1668 HCU at Bottesford in late Nov '44 meeting up with Lancasters Mk 1, 2 and 3, and finally to 514 Squadron, Waterbeach, on 2nd February '45. He was then aged just 22.

Peter's finely written account makes a fitting end to our story:

My crew and I were assigned to A Flight commanded then by Sqn Ldr K.G. Condict, DFC. The C.O. was Wing Commander P.L.B. Morgan, both of whom I remember as excellent officers. My first operation was a screened trip to Wesel, followed two days later by a trip with my full crew to the same target. Then followed a series of operations to a number of targets in the Ruhr and other places, and night operations, with the final operation to Bad Oldesloe on 24th April '45. I believe that this was the last operation carried out by 514 Squadron on bombing operations. On 30th April we took part in a food dropping mission to Rotterdam, and on May 2nd a similar food drop at

The Hague. On 14th May we flew to Juvincourt to uplift ex-prisoners of war, and on 17th, 18th and 23rd May we flew Belgian refugees to Brussels.

In retrospect, our short period spent with 514 Squadron was quite uneventful, bearing in mind the casualties and hazards suffered by some crews who had preceded us. We took some slight flak damage in the course of our short tour, had some fleeting Contact with enemy aircraft, enough to experience severe frights, but suffered no casualties.

All in all, our time on the Squadron seems to be very mundane compared with others, who appeared to be dogged with ill fortune. We watched with some interest the launching of V1 flying bombs from sites in France (by daylight) and the launch of V2 rockets towards London. I recall an incident which occurred at dispersal when we had run up our aircraft, and were about to return to the flight office by coach, when we heard a shout of alarm and looked up to see a 'cookie' which had fallen off a bomb trolley, and was rolling in our direction ! That put the wind up us for a while!

My life at Waterbeach was spent with my new wife in digs at Waterbeach awaiting the birth of our daughter. I vividly recall one day walking out with my wife near the village when we came across what I can only now recall as a 'hole in the wall' in a stone wall enclosing an order of nuns. My wife and I purchased a small quantity of honey from one of the nuns, who was permitted to speak to customers after ringing a bell or some such device to attract their attention. We were never able to see any part of the face, only the hands of the nun as she handed us our small purchase and change. On completing our purchase, the nun blessed us both, and this we found to be very touching and something that I shall remember for the rest of my life. Since my wife came from a town in Lancashire we were unable to have time enough to take leave away from Waterbeach, and so we spent a good deal of time visiting Cambridge and lazy afternoons on the Cam in a punt. Memories I shall cherish.

Returning on a particular daylight operation, I chose to formate on another aircraft to get in some practice rather than fly back separately. And so I spent all of the time on the trip back to base looking up close to the rear gunner of the aircraft I was following. It was a lovely sunny afternoon and everything appeared to be normal. We were not allowed to maintain radio contact with each other, and therefore had no idea that Condict's aircraft had been hit by a large piece of flak, which had severed the head of his wireless operator, who was also the signals leader of 'A' Flight. It was only after we had taxied into dispersal after landing and saw an ambulance in attendance on the Squadron Leader's aircraft and a body being removed, that we realised that a tragedy had occurred to that crew.

My thoughts return to those days when one's name appeared on the battle order with time of briefing etc., and a meal of real eggs and bacon with real milk served to those crews participating, then the briefing itself, followed by transport out to dispersal and the waiting ground crews, negotiating the dreaded main spar to the cockpit, the green light from the tower for startup, and the long taxi out to the duty pilot's caravan parked near the end of the runway, and the throng of people assembled to wave good byes to all of us in turn, some of whom never to make it back. Then the take-off itself, always a moment of tension with the knowledge that an engine could fail on take-off, and then the marvellous sensation of lift-off and acceleration with the undercarriage coming up and the climb out to join up with others for the trip out, and, hopefully, back. The climb to altitude and designated turning points, many of which took us over parts of London where we could be seen and heard from the ground, then crossing the coast outbound and crossing the enemy coast ahead, at night the all-pervading darkness and the occasional turbulence from aircraft ahead, daytime with vapour trails enhancing the sky and the comforting sight of escorting fighters above and below. Then reaching the initial point with all alert for the impending attack and the burst of flak, seemingly harmless until one could see the flame within the bursts, and concentration on the bombing run, and the relief with "bombs away", then turning away for the run home, coffee and biscuits all round when well clear of the area, but still alert for friendly aircraft sliding too close for comfort.

Crossing the coast of dear old England, and at night identifying the numerous airfield beacons and finally Waterbeach and the Drem system used to guide us in. By day, calling up the tower for landing instructions and finally the landing and taxiing to dispersal. The coach ride to de-briefing and the rum laced coffee, time to relax a little and a short chat to the de-briefing Waaf Officer, a word of encouragement from the Wing Commander Flying, and perhaps a word from some Brass Hat from Bomber Command. These memories will always endure, as they will for all who were fortunate to survive a tour, or even a partial tour, with Bomber Command. My short and uninteresting tale has been told many times before by crews with much more experience than I was able to assemble for the telling. My thoughts go out to all old friends, many of whom long since gone, with whom I had the honour to serve. I will always remember them.

Please excuse the ramblings of an old aviator. I hope that some of those who may choose to read this account of my short term with 514 Squadron may be amused by the telling of such quaint goings-on many years ago.

Operation Manna

by Eric Basford, Fitter, A Flight.

Throughout April '45, reports indicated that in parts of Western Holland still under occupation, the Dutch civilians were desperately short of food. Many were dying from malnutrition, but the German C in C refused to allow any food to reach them from the surrounding areas that had been liberated. It had been rumoured that negotiations were underway between the RAF and the German Commander of West Holland with a View to supplying the Dutch with food by air.

After several false hopes, the obstacles were overcome and 514 was one of many Squadrons scheduled to take part in 'Operation Manna'. The food was packed in hessian sacks, secured within the bomb bay by means of a double canvas door arrangement. Most of the food was in dried form and would have to be reconstituted.

514's dropping zone was near the Hague. The German's had specified the flight path, directly over their flak batteries, and also the height. Many of the crews were apprehensive of such an arrangement. They had to fly straight and low with bomb doors open, and at the dropping point, trigger the canvas doors to release the sacks of food. The crews returned in good spirits, having flown at low level over the top of the flak defences and observed the gunners in position, but there were no incidents. They said the whole population seemed to be there to greet them with much cheering and waving. Horses and carts, wheelbarrows and trolleys of various kinds had been drawn up ready to move the food. Several other drops were made that day in West Holland. Next day there was a repeat operation, but this time 514's dropping zone was near Rotterdam, with the same ecstatic reception from the Dutch. These operations continued for a little while, but as the German Commanders were surrendering one after the other, food supplies were able to move in by road and the food drops by air were terminated.

514 Squadron Roll of Honour

Rank	Forename	Surname	Role	Aircraft	Operation	Date	Age
/O	Thomas	Adams	B/Aimer	LM286	Homberg	20/11/1944	28
gt	Lawrence	Adkin	Navigator	DS706	Berlin	30/01/1944	21
/O	Stanley	Anderson	Pilot	HK571	Homberg	21/07/1944	23
gt	Frederick	Ansell	M/U Gnr	LL690	Valenciennes	16/06/1944	34
/S	William	Anthony	Wireless Op	HK570	Homberg	21/07/1944	
/O	Leonard	Arkless	Pilot	LM277	Calais	20/09/1944	24
gt	Cyril	Atter	Wireless Op	NG350	Osterfeld	11/12/1944	21
/O	Paul	Bailey	Navigator	DS787	Kamen	11/09/1944	20
gt	Keith	Baker	M/U Gnr	DS818	Gelsenkirchen	13/06/1944	
gt	William	Baker	B/Aimer	LL627	Magdeburg	22/01/1944	22
/S	William	Ball	B/Aimer	DS823	Leipzig	20/02/1944	30
gt	John	Balman	M/U Gnr	NG350	Osterfeld	11/12/1944	19
gt	Clive	Banfield	F/Engineer	LL639	Aachen	11/04/1944	
gt	John	Barker	M/U Gnr	LL680	Magdeburg	21/01/1944	19
/O	Kenneth	Barker	B/Aimer	PD265	Homberg	21/11/1944	
/S	Roger	Basey	B/Aimer	LL671	Berlin	24/12/1943	20
gt	William	Bates	B/Aimer	LL681	Leipzig	20/02/1944	23
/O	Donald	Beaton	Pilot	RF230	Exodus	09/05/1945	22
/O	Frederick	Beers	Navigator	PB185	Stuttgart	25/07/1944	26
Sgt	Albert	Benham	Wireless Op	LL678	Gelsenkirchen	13/06/1944	21
Sgt	Alfred	Bennett	F/Engineer	DS823	Leipzig	20/02/1944	20
Sgt	Philip	Bennett	F/Engineer	LL625	Berlin	24/03/1944	19
/O	Richard	Bennett	B/Aimer	DS813	Stuttgart	29/07/1944	21
F/S	Richard	Bennett	Pilot	LL627	Magdeburg	22/01/1944	20
P/O	Bertil	Bergquist	M/U Gnr	DS785	Schweinfurt	25/02/1944	22
LAC	Derrick	Bichard	Radar Mech		Waterbeach	29/12/1944	20
Sgt	Jack	Birch	Rear Gunner	DS781	Duisburg	22/05/1944	22
Sgt	Arthur	Bird	M/U Gnr	DS817	Frankfurt	20/12/1943	23

Some of the Story of 514 Squadron

F/S	Henry	Bishop	M/U Gnr	PB906	Wanne-Eickel	17/01/1945
Sgt	Joseph	Black	F/Engineer	LL690	Valenciennes	16/06/1944
Sgt	Leonard	Blackford	Rear Gunner	LL703	Frankfurt	23/03/1944
Sgt	Arthur	Blackshaw	Wireless Op	NN772	Wiesbaden	02/02/1945
Sgt	William	Blake	M/U Gnr	LL731	Frankfurt	12/09/1944
F/S	Benjamin	Bloom	Wireless Op	LL690	Valenciennes	16/06/1944
Sgt	William	Blore	M/U Gnr	ME858	Homberg	21/07/1944
Sgt	Arthur	Blunden	F/Engineer	LL641	Le Mans	20/05/1944
F/S	John	Boanson	M/U Gnr	DS822	Massy Palaiseau	08/06/1944
F/S	Derek	Bolton	Wireless Op	LM684	Homberg	21/11/1944
LAC	Samuel	Bolton	Flight Mech		Waterbeach	29/12/1944
F/O	William	Bonell	Navigator	LL733	Caen	30/07/1944
Sgt	Alfred	Booth	M/U Gnr	PB185	Stuttgart	25/07/1944
Sgt	Leslie	Bostock	F/Engineer	LL671	Berlin	24/12/1943
F/O	Philip	Boulter	F/Engineer	LL685	Brunswick	14/01/1944
Sgt	Alan	Bowen	Rear Gunner	NG350	Osterfeld	11/12/1944
F/L	George	Boyd	Pilot	DS706	Berlin	30/01/1944
Sgt	Alfred	Braine	Rear Gunner	LM206	Stuttgart	29/07/1944
Sgt	James	Brent	Navigator	DS784	Mannheim	18/11/1943
Sgt	Arthur	Brettell	M/U Gnr	LL627	Magdeburg	22/01/1944
AC2	Donald	Brewer	Arm't Asst		Waterbeach	29/12/1944
F/O	William	Brickwood	Pilot	LL731	Frankfurt	12/09/1944
F/S	John	Brittain	Wireless Op	RF230	J Exodus	09/05/1945
F/S	Reginald	Bromley	Rear Gunner	LL639	Aachen	11/04/1944
Sgt	Cyril	Brown	Rear Gunner	PB185	Stuttgart	25/07/1944
F/O	David	Brown	Navigator	ME858	Homberg	21/07/1944
Sgt	George	Brown	Wireless Op	DS818	Gelsenkirchen	13/06/1944
W/O	William	Brown	B/Aimer	DS781	Duisburg	22/05/1944
W/O	Kenneth	Bryan	Wireless Op	DS822	Massy Palaiseau	08/06/1944
F/O	Harold	Bryant	M/U Gnr	LL732	Chambly	02/05/1944
F/S	James	Bryson	Navigator	PB906	Wanne-Eickel	17/01/1945

gt	George	Bumstead	F/Engineer	LM181	Homberg	21/07/1944	19
/O	Arnold	Burgess	B/Aimer	PB185	Stuttgart	25/07/1944	20
gt	Anthony	Buttling	Rear Gunner	DS669	Dusseldorf	23/04/1944	
gt	Lawrence	Buxton	Wireless Op	DS633	Duisburg	22/05/1944	22
gt	Robert	Byth	M/U Gnr	LL698	Nuremburg	31/03/1944	
/S	Colin	Campbell	M/U Gnr	DS828	Dusseldorf	23/04/1944	19
/O	Maurice	Cantin	Pilot	DS814	Berlin	26/11/1943	21
gt	Harold	Carter	F/Engineer	DS813	Stuttgart	29/07/1944	
gt	William	Casey	Wireless Op	LL671	Berlin	24/12/1943	22
/O	Henry	Chapman	M/U Gnr	DS813	Stuttgart	29/07/1944	
/S	Wilbur	Chapman	Wireless Op	DS824	Magdeburg	26/01/1944	26
/O	Thomas	Charlton	Pilot	PB143	Stettin	30/08/1944	21
/L	George	Chequer	Pilot	DS735	Berlin	30/01/1944	22
gt	Victor	Childs	Rear Gunner	LL691	English Channel	01/05/1944	19
/L	Walter	Chitty	Pilot	LL733	Caen	30/07/1944	23
gt	Cecil	Clarke	M/U Gnr	LL728	Kiel	26/08/1944	29
gt	Frank	Clarke	B/Aimer	NN775	Gelsenkirchen	05/03/1945	
/O	Ronald	Clements	2nd Pilot	DS725	Leipzig	20/10/1943	27
/S	Robert	Cole	Wireless Op	LL732	Chambly	02/05/1944	
gt	Eric	Coles	F/Engineer	LL620	Villers Bocage	30/06/1944	
gt	Leslie	Coles	Rear Gunner	PD265	Homberg	21/11/1944	20
/S	Ronald	Collender	Wireless Op	LL731	Frankfurt	12/09/1944	21
gt	Thomas	Combe	M/U Gnr	LL733	Dortmund	22/05/1944	19
/S	Patrick	Constable	Navigator	DS828	Dusseldorf	23/04/1944	33
gt	Alfred	Cooke	Rear Gunner	LL698	Nuremburg	31/03/1944	19
gt /O	Bernard	Cooper	M/U Gnr	HK570	Homberg	21/07/1944	19
gt	Gilbert	Cosgrove	F/Engineer	LL653	Stuttgart	16/03/1944	22
/O	Reginald	Cowles	Navigator	NG350	Osterfeld	11/12/1944	23
gt	Kenneth	Cragg	B/Aimer	DS736	Leipzig	20/02/1944	22
/O	Harold	Crampton	B/Aimer	LL697	Lens	11/08/1944	26

P/O	Donald	Crombie	Pilot	DS836	Nuremburg	31/03/1944
Sgt	Robert	Curle	Rear Gunner	DS738	Berlin	02/12/1943
F/L	Robert	Curtis	Pilot	LL732	Chambly	02/05/1944
F/O	James	Daly	Navigator	DS813	Stuttgart	29/07/1944
LAC	Ronald	Davies	Flight Mech		Waterbeach	29/12/1944
Sgt	Daniel	Davis	Rear Gunner	LL690	Valenciennes	16/06/1944
Sgt	Richard	Day	Wireless Op	LL684	Frankfurt	22/03/1944
P/O	Herbert	Delacour	Pilot	LL678	Gelsenkirchen	13/06/1944
F/O	Ronald	Dell	Wireless Op	PB143	Stettin	30/08/1944
Sgt	Norman	Derham	F/Engineer	ME858	Homberg	21/07/1944
Sgt	Peter	Devlin	M/U Gnr	PB143	Stettin	30/08/1944
Sgt	Ronald	Digby	M/U Gnr	LM181	Homberg	21/07/1944
F/S	Arthur	Dimock	B/Aimer	LL679	Brunswick	14/01/1944
W/O	Leslie	Ding	B/Aimer	LL733	Caen	30/07/1944
F/S	Thomas	Dodd	Navigator	LL627	Magdeburg	22/01/1944
W/O	James	Dodding	2nd Pilot	LL681	Leipzig	20/02/1944
P/O	Hilary	Doherty	Rear Gunner	LL620	Villers Bocage	30/06/1944
Sgt	Frank	Dolamore	F/Engineer	DS781	Duisburg	22/05/1944
Sgt	John	Dowding	Wireless Op	DS706	Berlin	30/01/1944
F/O	Alan	Downward	Navigator	LM685	Dortmund-Huckarde	03/02/1945
Sgt	Kenneth	Drummond	2nd Pilot	LL653	Stuttgart	16/03/1944
Sgt	James	Dunbar	B/Aimer	DS633	Duisburg	22/05/1944
Sgt	Malcom	Duncan	Rear Gunner	LM181	Homberg	21/07/1944
F/S	Thomas	Durie	Wireless Op	LM181	Homberg	21/07/1944
W/O2	Richard	Eason	B/Aimer	LL691	English Channel	01/05/1944
F/S	Desmond	Edwards	Navigator	LL671	Berlin	24/12/1943
W/O	James	Edwards	Wireless Op	LL728	Kiel	26/08/1944
F/S	Arthur	Elliott	Wireless Op	DS815	Frankfurt	23/03/1944
F/S	Orval	Evers	Rear Gunner	RF230	Juvincourt - Ford	09/05/1945
Sgt	Leslie	Eyre	M/U Gnr	DS814	Berlin	26/11/1943

Lancasters at Waterbeach

gt	John	Fenwick	Navigator	DS785	Schweinfurt	25/02/1944	21
gt	Thomas	Fenwick	B/Aimer	LM735	Emmerich	07/10/1944	
/O	Harold	Fidge	Rear Gunner	LL681	Leipzig	20/02/1944	29
/O	Warren	Fisher	Pilot	LM685	Dortmund-Huckarde	03/02/1945	
/O	Leslie	Flack	Pilot	ME365	Salzbergen	06/03/1945	25
gt	Ronald	Fontaine	B/Aimer	DS784	Mannheim	18/11/1943	
/L	Alba	Fowke	Pilot	DS813	Stuttgart	29/07/1944	26
gt	Kenneth	Fox	F/Engineer	PB178	Villers Bocage	30/06/1944	20
gt	Kenneth	Foyle	F/Engineer	LL680	Magdeburg	21/01/1944	19
gt	James	Fraser	F/Engineer	DS633	Duisburg	22/05/1944	27
gt	Alexander	Freeburn	Navigator	DS633	Duisburg	22/05/1944	28
gt	Sanford	Frith	F/Engineer	LL698	Nuremburg	31/03/1944	19
gt	J	Gallagher	Rear Gunner	DS633	Duisburg	22/05/1944	19
/S	James	Gallagher	Navigator	LL679	Brunswick	14/01/1944	22
gt	Leslie	Gardiner	Rear Gunner	LL680	Magdeburg	21/01/1944	
gt	Andrew	George	M/U Gnr	PB178	Villers Bocage	30/06/1944	30
/O	Matthew	George	Wireless Op	LM286	Homberg	20/11/1944	23
/O	Walter	Gibbs	Rear Gunner	PB143	Stettin	30/08/1944	36
/S	Thomas	Gibson	Pilot	DS633	Duisburg	21/05/1944	22
/O	Robert	Giffin	2nd Pilot	LL692	Stuttgart	29/07/1944	
/O	Thomas	Gilchrist	Pilot	LM735	Emmerich	07/10/1944	21
gt	Richard	Gill	Rear Gunner	LL652	Aachen	28/05/1944	35
gt	Harry	Glansford	B/Aimer	ME858	Homberg	21/07/1944	23
gt	Ernest	Gledhill	Wireless Op	DS682	Dusseldorf	23/04/1944	22
gt	Geoffrey	Goddard	B/Aimer	DS828	Dusseldorf	23/04/1944	23
/O	Osmond	Goddard	Wireless Op	LL738	Nuremburg	31/03/1944	20
gt	Kenneth	Goodman	B/Aimer	PB143	Stettin	30/08/1944	21
gt	Peter	Gosnold	F/Engineer	PD265	Homberg	21/11/1944	20
/S	Wallace	Granbois	Rear Gunner	DS828	Dusseldorf	23/04/1944	26
/S	Robert	Gray	Navigator	LM286	Homberg	20/11/1944	

Some of the Story of 514 Squadron

F/S	Alan	Green	Navigator	DS682	Dusseldorf	23/04/1944
F/S	Bryan	Green	B/Aimer	LL732	Chambly	02/05/1944
F/S	Frederick	Gregory	Pilot	LL698	Nuremburg	31/03/1944
F/S	Frank	Guest	B/Aimer	NG350	Osterfeld	11/12/1944
Sgt	Charles	Guy	F/Engineer	LL733	Caen	30/07/1944
F/S	Robert	Guy	Rear Gunner	DS822	Massy Palaiseau	08/06/1944
F/S	Ernest	Hack	F/Engineer	HK570	Homberg	21/07/1944
Sgt	Ernest	Haigh	M/U Gnr	DS781	Duisburg	22/05/1944
W/O	John	Hall	Wireless Op	DS787	Kamen	11/09/1944
F/S	Norman	Hall	Pilot	DS736	Leipzig	20/02/1944
W/O	Raymond	Hall	Rear Gunner	LL732	Chambly	02/05/1944
F/O	Herbert	Hallam	Navigator	LM684	Homberg	21/11/1944
F/S	Jack	Hannesson	Pilot	PB178	Villers Bocage	30/06/1944
Sgt	Ronald	Harding	Wireless Op	PD265	Homberg	21/11/1944
F/S	Ronald	Hardy	Wireless Op	LM685	Dortmund-Huckarde	03/02/1945
F/O	John	Harland	Pilot	LM286	Homberg	20/11/1944
Sgt	J	Harman	M/U Gnr	LM277	Calais	20/09/1944
P/O	John	Harrison	Pilot	DS669	Dusseldorf	23/04/1944
Sgt	Robert	Harrison	Rear Gunner	DS785	Schweinfurt	25/02/1944
Sgt	William	Harvey	Rear Gunner	NN772	Wiesbaden	14/01/1944
P/O	William	Harvey	Wireless Op	LL685	Brunswick	02/02/1945
LAC	Geoffrey	Hayden	Radar Mech		Waterbeach	29/12/1944
Sgt	Herbert	Hayward	Rear Gunner	DS682	Dusseldorf	23/04/1944
F/O	Frank	Hebditch	Pilot	LL728	Kiel	26/08/1944
Sgt	Dennis	Heeley	Rear Gunner	ME365	Salzbergen	06/03/1945
F/S	Clement	Henn	M/U Gnr	LL639	Aachen	11/04/1944
Sgt	John	Hennis	Rear Gunner	LL679	Brunswick	14/01/1944
P/O	Walter	Henry	Pilot	DS823	Leipzig	20/02/1944
F/O	Donald	Henshaw	B/Aimer	DS824	Magdeburg	22/01/1944
Sgt	Kenneth	Heron	Wireless Op	LL620	Villers Bocage	30/06/1944

Lancasters at Waterbeach

/O	Ray	Hilchey	Navigator	RF230	Exodus	09/05/1945	22
/O	Ellis	Hill	Pilot	NG350	Osterfeld	11/12/1944	
/O	Frederick	Hill	M/U Gnr	LL652	Aachen	28/05/1944	26
gt	Harold	Hill	Rear Gunner	DS836	Nuremburg	31/03/1944	20
gt	Arthur	Hodson	F/Engineer	DS736	Leipzig	20/02/1944	20
gt	Christopher	Hogg	M/U Gnr	NN775	Gelsenkirchen	05/03/1945	20
gt	Arthur	Holmes	M/U Gnr	DS816	Valenciennes	16/06/1944	
gt	George	Holt	Wireless Op	ME858	Homberg	21/07/1944	22
gt	Allan	Hope	B/Aimer	HK570	Homberg	21/07/1944	23
gt	George	Hubbard	B/Aimer	DS787	Kamen	11/09/1944	
F/S	John	Hudson	Pilot	DS828	Dusseldorf	23/04/1944	22
W/O	Dennis	Hughes	Rear Gunner	LL627	Magdeburg	22/01/1944	22
P/O	Garth	Hughes	Pilot	LL738	Nuremburg	31/03/1944	25
Sgt	Patrick	Hughes	Wireless Op	LL639	Aachen	11/04/1944	
F/S	Raymond	Hutt	Navigator	LL690	Valenciennes	16/06/1944	
F/O	George	Jacobson	B/Aimer	DS682	Dusseldorf	23/04/1944	27
Sgt	Kenneth	Jeffery	M/U Gnr	HK571	Homberg	21/07/1944	20
F/S	Edward	Jenner	M/U Gnr	LL733	Caen	30/07/1944	21
Sgt	Howell	John	Rear Gunner	LL684	Frankfurt	22/03/1944	
Sgt	Albert	Johnson	F/Engineer	LL684	Frankfurt	22/03/1944	20
F/S	Frank	Jones	Wireless Op	LM206	Stuttgart	29/07/1944	22
Sgt	Graham	Jones	F/Engineer	DS828	Dusseldorf	23/04/1944	
F/L	Robert	Jones	Pilot	LM206	Stuttgart	29/07/1944	21
F/O	Stanley	Jones	Rear Gunner	LL728	Kiel	26/08/1944	30
F/S	Thomas	Jones	Wireless Op	PB185	Stuttgart	25/07/1944	22
Sgt	Thomas	Jones	Wireless Op	LM277	Calais	20/09/1944	
F/O	William	Jones	Navigator	LL732	Chambly	02/05/1944	35
Sgt	Alfred	Kay	Pilot	DS785	Schweinfurt	25/02/1944	
Sgt	James	Keenen	F/Engineer	DS824	Magdeburg	22/01/1944	
F/S	Lancelot	Kell	Wireless Op	LL679	Brunswick	14/01/1944	29
Sgt	George	Kemp	M/U Gnr	DS633	Duisburg	22/05/1944	30

Sgt	Douglas	Kenny	M/U Gnr	DS823	Leipzig	20/02/1944	
F/O	Holman	Kerr	Pilot	NN775	Gelsenkirchen	05/03/1945	
Sgt	Donald	Kilner	B/Aimer	LL653	Stuttgart	16/03/1944	
Sgt	Kerry	King	F/Engineer	DS814	Berlin	26/11/1943	
Cpl	William	King			Circs not stated	22/05/1944	
P/O	Ernest	Kingham	Pilot	LL690	Valenciennes	16/06/1944	
F/L	Leonard	Kingwell	Pilot	LL681	Leipzig	20/02/1944	
F/S	Roy	Kirkpatrick	B/Aimer	DS669	Dusseldorf	23/04/1944	
Sgt	George	Knight	Navigator	LL681	Leipzig	20/02/1944	
Sgt	Henry	Knight	F/Engineer	LM735	Emmerich	07/10/1944	
F/S	Jack	Knights	B/Aimer	LL625	Berlin	24/03/1944	2
F/O	John	Laing	Pilot	LL625	Berlin	24/03/1944	2
Sgt	Ronald	Laishley	F/Engineer	LL679	Brunswick	14/01/1944	1
Sgt	William	Lamond	F/Engineer	LL691	English Channel	01/05/1944	2
F/S	Ernest	Lane	Rear Gunner	DS824	Magdeburg	22/01/1944	
Sgt	Robert	Lane	M/U Gnr	LM206	Stuttgart	29/07/1944	3
F/S	Robert	Langford	Wireless Op	DS781	Duisburg	22/05/1944	2
Sgt	William	Lannigan	Rear Gunner	DS823	Leipzig	20/02/1944	2
W/O	William	Larmouth	Navigator	HK571	Homberg	21/07/1944	2
W/O	John	Lassam	Pilot	HK570	Homberg	21/07/1944	2
F/S	John	Lawrie	Pilot	LM180	Russelsheim	13/08/1944	2
Sgt	Bernard	Le Neve-Foster	F/Engineer	LL645	Frankfurt	22/03/1944	22
AC1	Harry	Leach	Electrician		Waterbeach	29/12/1944	34
F/S	Beverley	Lee	Navigator	PB178	Villers Bocage	30/06/1944	31
Sgt	Frank	Lewis	Wireless Op	DS736	Leipzig	20/02/1944	24
F/S	Gordon	Lewis	Navigator	DS818	Gelsenkirchen	13/06/1944	23
F/O	Ronald	Limbert	Pilot	LM684	Homberg	21/11/1944	22
F/O	Kenneth	Loder	B/Aimer	LM206	Stuttgart	29/07/1944	21
Sgt	Harold	Long	Rear Gunner	ME858	Homberg	21/07/1944	20
F/O	Francis	Longston	Navigator	LL620	Villers Bocage	30/06/1944	22

Lancasters at Waterbeach

gt	Edward	Lowe	Navigator	LL680	Magdeburg	21/01/1944	
gt	Kenneth	Lowery	F/Engineer	LL627	Magdeburg	22/01/1944	20
gt	Stanley	Lucas	M/U Gnr	LM286	Homberg	20/11/1944	
/O	Alan	Lundie	B/Aimer	LM684	Homberg	21/11/1944	
/O	James	Lupton	Rear Gunner	LL731	Frankfurt	12/09/1944	20
gt	Clarence	MacKenzie	M/U Gnr	LL696	Nuremburg	31/03/1944	19
/O	Donald	Manchul	Rear Gunner	HK570	Homberg	21/07/1944	
/O	Gerald	Manlow	Navigator	LM735	Emmerich	07/10/1944	24
gt	Edward	Marchant	F/Engineer	DS785	Schweinfurt	25/02/1944	20
gt	William	Marsden	F/Engineer	NN775	Gelsenkirchen	05/03/1945	20
gt	Reginald	Marshall	Wireless Op	LL641	Le Mans	20/05/1944	22
/O	John	Martin	Navigator	LL685	Brunswick	14/01/1944	
gt	Stanley	Martin	F/Engineer	LL732	Chambly	02/05/1944	32
/S	Peter	Martindale	B/Aimer	DS706	Berlin	30/01/1944	23
/S	Paul	Mason	Pilot	LL679	Brunswick	14/01/1944	23
gt	Joseph	Masson	M/U Gnr	LL641	Le Mans	20/05/1944	
/O	Merlin	Matkin	2nd pilot	PB906	Wanne-Eickel	17/01/1945	21
gt	Frederick	Maunder	F/Engineer	NN772	Wiesbaden	02/02/1945	19
gt	John	McCormick	Wireless Op	DS785	Schweinfurt	25/02/1944	20
/S	James	McCreary	B/Aimer	LL698	Nuremburg	31/03/1944	20
gt	James	McGahey	F/Engineer	DS836	Nuremburg	31/03/1944	
/S	Anthony	McGlone	Wireless Op	PB906	Wanne-Eickel	17/01/1945	23
/S	William	McIlRaith	B/Aimer	LM181	Homberg	21/07/1944	27
/S	William	McIntosh	Navigator	LM265	Russelsheim	13/08/1944	25
gt	John	McKeown	B/Aimer	DS785	Schweinfurt	25/02/1944	20
/O	Lamont	McLean	Pilot	LM181	Homberg	21/07/1944	23
/S	Stanley	McLean	Wireless Op	LM735	Emmerich	07/10/1944	20
/O	William	McLean	Pilot	NN772	Wiesbaden	02/02/1945	25
gt	Charles	McLoughlin	B/Aimer	LL680	Magdeburg	21/01/1944	
/S	Alfred	McMurrugh	F/Engineer	RF230	Exodus	09/05/1945	23
gt	John	McNeil	M/U Gnr	DS813	Stuttgart	15/03/1944	27

Sgt	Peter	McQueeney	F/Engineer	LL672	Magdeburg	21/01/1944	
Sgt	Albert	McWhinney	M/U Gnr	LM685	Dortmund-Huckarde	03/02/1945	
Sgt	William	Michell	Wireless Op	DS814	Berlin	26/11/1943	
F/O	Thomas	Middleton	Pilot	PB185	Stuttgart	25/07/1944	
F/O	Douglas	Millar	Pilot	ME858	Homberg	21/07/1944	
F/S	Leslie	Millis	Navigator	DS824	Magdeburg	22/01/1944	
Sgt	Reginald	Mirams	M/U Gnr	DS706	Berlin	30/01/1944	
Sgt	Robert	Montgomery	Wireless Op	DS735	Berlin	30/01/1944	
Sgt	Harry	Morgan	Rear Gunner	PB178	Villers Bocage	30/06/1944	
F/O	Maurice	Morgan-Owen	Pilot	DS682	Dusseldorf	23/04/1944	
Sgt	Hugh	Morris	Wireless Op	DS817	Frankfurt	20/12/1943	
P/O	Alfred	Morrison	Rear Gunner	LM685	Dortmund-Huckarde	03/02/1945	3
W/O	Kenneth	Mortimer	Navigator	LL735	Berlin	19/04/1945	2
F/S	John	Moulsdale	B/Aimer	LL639	Aachen	11/04/1944	3
F/O	Gordon	Murphy	Rear Gunner	DS813	Stuttgart	29/07/1944	2
Sgt	Frederick	Nash	Wireless Op	DS669	Dusseldorf	23/04/1944	2
Sgt	Per	Nelson	Rear Gunner	LL671	Berlin	24/12/1943	2.
Sgt	Dennis	Newbury	F/Engineer	LL681	Leipzig	20/02/1944	
F/S	Stanley	Newman	Wireless Op	LL652	Aachen	28/05/1944	2
Sgt	Alexander	Nicholson	Rear Gunner	DS706	Berlin	30/01/1944	25
F/S	Norman	Nightingale	Navigator	NN772	Wiesbaden	02/02/1945	22
Sgt	Ronald	Norris	F/Engineer	DS669	Dusseldorf	23/04/1944	
Sgt	Ernest	Oakley	M/U Gnr	LL679	Brunswick	14/01/1944	
F/S	John	O'Brien	M/U Gnr	DS735	Berlin	30/01/1944	23
Sgt	Walter	O'Dea	Rear Gunner	DS817	Frankfurt	20/12/1943	20
F/S	Patrick	O'Donohue	Wireless Op	ME365	Salzbergen	06/03/1945	21
F/S	Allan	Olsen	Wireless Op	NN775	Gelsenkirchen	05/03/1945	21
F/O	George	Orr	Pilot	PB906	Wanne-Eickel	17/01/1945	34
Sgt	Henry	Osborn	F/Engineer	DS816	Valenciennes	16/06/1944	20
Sgt	Thomas	Owen	Wireless Op	LL653	Stuttgart	16/03/1944	21

Lancasters at Waterbeach

/O	Ian	Partington	Navigator	LM277	Calais	20/09/1944	23
gt	Robert	Paterson	F/Engineer	LM286	Homberg	20/11/1944	19
gt	Allen	Pattison	B/Aimer	LL645	Nuremburg	31/03/1944	23
gt	Claude	Payne	M/U Gnr	DS836	Nuremburg	31/03/1944	34
gt	Kenneth	Peake	M/U Gnr	LL653	Stuttgart	16/03/1944	
/O	Kaiho	Penkuri	Pilot	LL653	Stuttgart	16/03/1944	21
/O	Samuel	Phillips	2nd Pilot	LL678	Gelsenkirchen	13/06/1944	
/O	Roy	Picton	Navigator	LL678	Gelsenkirchen	13/06/1944	
gt	Sydney	Picton	Wireless Op	DS813	Stuttgart	29/07/1944	21
gt	Edward	Pitman	Wireless Op	LL680	Magdeburg	21/01/1944	21
gt	Joseph	Plant	F/Engineer	LL728	Kiel	26/08/1944	35
gt	Reginald	Pomroy	F/Engineer	PB143	Stettin	30/08/1944	23
gt	Eric	Pond	Wireless Op	LL698	Nuremburg	31/03/1944	
gt	John	Porrelli	Rear Gunner	DS816	Valenciennes	16/06/1944	35
gt	Arthur	Pratt	M/U Gnr	DS824	Magdeburg	22/01/1944	
gt	Albert	Prescott	M/U Gnr	LM684	Homberg	21/11/1944	22
/S	Charles	Prowles	Pilot	DS816	Valenciennes	16/06/1944	21
gt	Norman	Readman	F/Engineer	NG350	Osterfeld	11/12/1944	
gt	Andrew	Reilly	M/U Gnr	ME365	Salzbergen	06/03/1945	21
gt	Kenneth	Rhodes	B/Aimer	HK571	Homberg	21/07/1944	
/O	Ivor	Rich	Navigator	LL684	Frankfurt	22/03/1944	35
/S	Edgar	Richardson	Pilot	LM265	Russelsheim	13/08/1944	20
/S	John	Richardson	Wireless Op	LL733	Caen	30/07/1944	21
gt	Stanley	Ricketts	Navigator	DS823	Leipzig	20/02/1944	20
AC2	Charles	Riman			Circs not stated	09/09/1944	19
gt	Bleddyn	Roberts	M/U Gnr	LM735	Emmerich	07/10/1944	
gt	Eric	Roberts	Navigator	DS817	Frankfurt	20/12/1943	21
F/S	Cecil	Robertshaw	Wireless Op	LM265	Russelsheim	13/08/1944	
AC1	George	Robinson	Passenger	LL691	English Channel	01/05/1944	
Sgt	Alan	Roderick	F/Engineer	LL652	Aachen	28/05/1944	24
W/O	Henry	Rolph	Wireless Op	DS828	Dusseldorf	23/04/1944	24

Some of the Story of 514 Squadron

P/O	Henry	Roome	2nd Pilot	LM265	Russelsheim	13/08/1944	
Sgt	Charles	Rose	M/U Gnr	LL695	Duisburg	22/05/1944	
P/O	Frank	Rosher	Rear Gunner	LL685	Brunswick	14/01/1944	
Sgt	William	Saddler	Navigator	DS814	Berlin	26/11/1943	
Sgt	Henry	Sadler	F/Engineer	DS682	Dusseldorf	23/04/1944	
Sgt	Charles	Salt	Rear Gunner	LL625	Berlin	24/03/1944	
Sgt	Charles	Samson	Rear Gunner	HK571	Homberg	21/07/1944	
F/S	George	Savage	Rear Gunner	LL678	Gelsenkirchen	13/06/1944	
F/S	Gerald	Scott	Wireless Op	LL625	Berlin	24/03/1944	
Sgt	Roger	Scott	F/Engineer	LM684	Homberg	21/11/1944	
Sgt	Anthony	Sealtiel	F/Engineer	LL695	Duisburg	22/05/1944	1
Sgt	Reginald	Seddon	B/Aimer	DS817	Frankfurt	20/12/1943	
F/S	Ernest	Shanks	B/Aimer	LL620	Villers Bocage	30/06/1944	
F/S	Edward	Shearing	Pilot	LL641	Le Mans	20/05/1944	2
Sgt	Patrick	Sheehy	Rear Gunner	LM735	Emmerich	07/10/1944	
Sgt	Joseph	Shepherd	M/U Gnr	LL645	Nuremburg	31/03/1944	1
Sgt	Robert	Shields	Rear Gunner	LM277	Calais	20/09/1944	
AC2	James	Simpson			Circs not stated	01/10/1944	2
F/O	Peter	Slater	M/U Gnr	PD265	Homberg	21/11/1944	
Sgt	Leonard	Slocombe	Rear Gunner	LM286	Homberg	20/11/1944	3
S/L	Ernest	Sly	Pilot	LL685	Brunswick	14/01/1944	
LAC	Laurence	Smales	Flight Mech		Waterbeach	29/12/1944	23
Sgt	James	Smethurst	F/Engineer	DS817	Frankfurt	20/12/1943	
F/S	Llewellyn	Smith	Navigator	LL738	Nuremburg	31/03/1944	26
Sgt	Philip	Smith	Rear Gunner	LM265	Russelsheim	13/08/1944	21
F/S	Sidney	Smith	Navigator	NN775	Gelsenkirchen	05/03/1945	21
Sgt	Stuart	Smith	B/Aimer	DS814	Berlin	26/11/1943	
F/O	James	Sneddon	M/U Gnr	LL685	Brunswick	14/01/1944	
F/S	William	Sparkes	Wireless Op	LM724	Hattingen	14/03/1945	23
F/S	Frank	Spencer	B/Aimer	LL690	Valenciennes	16/06/1944	19
F/S	George	Spencer	Rear Gunner	PB906	Wanne-Eickel	17/01/1945	32

/S	Ronald	Spencer	B/Aimer	DS816	Valenciennes	16/06/1944	29
/S	Keith	Stafford	Navigator	LL731	Frankfurt	12/09/1944	26
gt	Richard	Stafford	F/Engineer	PB185	Stuttgart	25/07/1944	
gt	Harry	Stagg	F/Engineer	DS784	Mannheim	18/11/1943	29
gt	William	Steger	Rear Gunner	DS818	Gelsenkirchen	13/06/1944	20
/O	Donald	Stephens	B/Aimer	LM685	Dortmund-Huckarde	03/02/1945	20
gt	Charlie	Stepney	Rear Gunner	LM684	Homberg	21/11/1944	30
gt	Norman	Stevens	Navigator	PB143	Stettin	30/08/1944	20
/S	Arthur	Stone	Navigator	LM181	Homberg	21/07/1944	22
/S	Gordon	Stromberg	Wireless Op	LL727	Massy Palaiseau	09/06/1944	19
Sgt	Raymond	Surtees	Wireless Op	DS816	Valenciennes	16/06/1944	
Sgt	William	Sutherland	Rear Gunner	LL653	Stuttgart	16/03/1944	32
Sgt	Harry	Taylor	M/U Gnr	LL681	Leipzig	20/02/1944	21
F/L	Lloyd	Taylor	Pilot	LL652	Aachen	21/07/1944	27
Sgt	Walter	Taylor	Navigator	HK570	Homberg	20/05/1944	35
F/S	Victor	Tayton	Navigator	LL641	Le Mans	20/05/1944	35
F/O	Alec	Teece	B/Aimer	LM277	Calais	20/09/1944	20
Sgt	Alfred	Tetley	M/U Gnr	DS682	Dusseldorf	23/04/1944	23
P/O	Noel	Thackray	Pilot	LL639	Aachen	11/04/1944	27
F/S	Cecil	Thomas	B/Aimer	LL652	Aachen	28/05/1944	23
P/O	Edwin	Thomas	B/Aimer	LL685	Brunswick	14/01/1944	28
Sgt	Frank	Thomas	Wireless Op	DS784	Mannheim	18/11/1943	
Sgt	Herbert	Thomas	Rear Gunner	NN775	Gelsenkirchen	05/03/1945	23
P/O	Stanley	Thomas	Pilot	DS784	Mannheim	18/11/1943	
Sgt	George	Thornton	Rear Gunner	LL738	Nuremburg	31/03/1944	22
W/O	Robert	Thornton	Pilot	DS787	Kamen	11/09/1944	22
F/S	Robert	Toms	M/U Gnr	RF230	Exodus	09/05/1945	20
Sgt	George	Trigwell	B/Aimer	LM265	Russelsheim	13/08/1944	21
F/S	Norman	Turner	Pilot	LL691	English Channel	01/05/1944	
Sgt	Morris	Tyler	Wireless Op	DS836	Nuremburg	31/03/1944	20

Some of the Story of 514 Squadron

Sgt	William	Udell	M/U Gnr	LL620	Villers Bocage	30/06/1944	
F/S	John	Underwood	Pilot	LL684	Frankfurt	22/03/1944	
F/S	Peter	Upton	Wireless Op	LL627	Magdeburg	22/01/1944	
Sgt	Francis	Vallance	Wireless Op	DS823	Leipzig	20/02/1944	
Sgt	Albert	Vickers	Navigator	LL625	Berlin	24/03/1944	
Sgt	Bernard	Vince	M/U Gnr	LM265	Russelsheim	13/08/1944	
Sgt	James	Vincent	Navigator	LL652	Aachen	28/05/1944	
F/S	Frederick	Wall	B/Aimer	ME365	Salzbergen	06/03/1945	
Sgt	Robert	Walne	Rear Gunner	DS814	Berlin	26/11/1943	
AC1	James	Ware			Circs not stated	12/01/1944	
F/S	William	Warr	F/Engineer	LM685	Dortmund-Huckarde	03/02/1945	
Sgt	Lewis	Warren	Rear Gunner	LL703	Frankfurt	23/03/1944	1
Sgt	Clifford	Washington	Navigator	LL728	Kiel	26/08/1944	
Sgt	William	Watkins	M/U Gnr	DS736	Leipzig	20/02/1944	2
LAC	Frederick	Watson	Flight Mech		Waterbeach	29/12/1944	2
Sgt	William	Watson	F/Engineer	ME365	Salzbergen	06/03/1945	
Sgt	Peter	Webb	F/Engineer	DS706	Berlin	30/01/1944	
F/S	George	Wells	Rear Gunner	LL733	Caen	30/07/1944	
Sgt	Roy	Werrill	F/Engineer	PB906	Wanne-Eickel	17/01/1945	
Sgt	Harry	West	F/Engineer	LL738	Nuremburg	31/03/1944	
Cpl	John	Westgarth			Waterbeach	29/12/1944	
Sgt	Percival	Whale	M/U Gnr	LL691	English Channel	01/05/1944	3
Sgt	Harold	Whichelow	Wireless Op	LL681	Leipzig	20/02/1944	33
F/S	Leslie	Whitbread	M/U Gnr	LL738	Nuremburg	31/03/1944	20
Sgt	Alan	White	F/Engineer	LM277	Calais	20/09/1944	20
Sgt	Raymond	Whitehall	Wireless Op	HK571	Homberg	21/07/1944	
Sgt	Augustine	Whitehead	Navigator	LL691	English Channel	01/05/1944	
P/O	Kenneth	Whitting	Pilot	LL671	Berlin	24/12/1943	25
F/S	Thomas	Wilcox	B/Aimer	PB906	Wanne-Eickel	17/01/1945	25
F/S	Edward	Wilde	Navigator	DS669	Dusseldorf	23/04/1944	23

166

gt	Benjamin	Williams	Rear Gunner	LL695	Duisburg	22/05/1944	20
gt	John	Williams	Navigator	DS736	Leipzig	20/02/1944	
/O	John	Williams	Pilot	DS824	Magdeburg	22/01/1944	
gt	Albert	Williston	Rear Gunner	LL672	Magdeburg	21/01/1944	27
gt	John	Wilson	F/Engineer	HK571	Homberg	21/07/1944	
gt	William	Wilson	M/U Gnr	DS669	Dusseldorf	23/04/1944	20
gt	Leo	Wilton	Rear Gunner	DS783	Berlin	02/12/1943	26
/O	Bernard	Windsor	Pilot	DS781	Duisburg	22/05/1944	29
gt	William	Winkley	Wireless Op	LL691	English Channel	01/05/1944	
gt	Thomas	Woodford	Rear Gunner	DS736	Leipzig	20/02/1944	
/O	Douglas	Woods	Pilot	LL620	Villers Bocage	30/06/1944	22
gt	Gordon	Woodward	Navigator	DS781	Duisburg	22/05/1944	
/O	Lawrence	Wry	Navigator	LL653	Stuttgart	16/03/1944	
/O	Roy	Young	Navigator	ME365	Salzbergen	06/03/1945	34

Evaders and Prisoners of War

In most Squadron aircraft shot down or otherwise lost, the majority of crew members died. This was mainly due to causes such as being directly hit by fighter fire or flak, the effects of fire or explosion, or, for crew members unable to make their escape, the ensuing crash of the falling aircraft. In aircraft lost, barely one in four crew members managed to successfully bale out and survive. Baling out over 'occupied Europe', alone and often at night, was extreme trauma. These members have experiences that most of us cannot share.

There was virtually no chance of help for aircrew who baled out over Germany. Their best hope was to be arrested without mishap and become a P.O.W. For crew members who came down over friendly territory such as France, Belgium and Holland, there was a fair possibility of receiving help from the ordinary but very brave inhabitants of these areas. If caught harbouring allied airmen these helpers faced the prospect of a death penalty as well as possible torture, or of being sent to a concentration camp where often they died.

Aircrew who received such assistance and weren't subsequently arrested to become prisoners of war, were termed 'Evaders'. Some were passed along clandestine 'escape routes', typically across France and over the Pyrenees into Spain, and thence back home to serve again. Others were sheltered in 'safe houses' or other places of assistance until such time as freedom arrived with the advancing allied armies.

Lancasters at Waterbeach

1k	Forename	Surname	Date	Aircraft	Operation	Role	Fate
	John	Alford	02-Dec-1943	DS738	Berlin	Bomb Aimer	POW
	Stuart	Baxter	03-Aug-1944	LL716	Bois de Cassan	Navigator	POW
	GH	Berridge	02-Feb-1945	NN772	Wiesbaden	MU Gunner	POW
	Joseph	Bourke	21-Jan-1944	LL672	Magdeburg	Pilot	POW
	HJ	Bourne	12-Jun-1944	DS818	Gelsenkirchen	Bomb Aimer	POW
	Reginald	Brailsford	11-May-1944	LL739	Louvain	Bomb Aimer	Evaded
	J	Brewer	21-Jan-1944	LL672	Magdeburg	MU Gunner	POW
	Fred	Brown	11-May-1944	LL739	Louvain	MU Gunner	POW
	Lindsay	Burford	12-Aug-1944	LM180	Russelsheim	MU Gunner	Evaded
	DR	Burns	11-Sep-1944	DS787	Kamen	Rear Gunner	POW
	Edward	Campbell	28-Jul-1944	LL692	Stuttgart	Pilot	Evaded
	Fred	Carey	07-Jun-1944	LL727	Massy Palaiseau	MU Gunner	POW
	J	Carey	30-Jan-1944	DS735	Berlin	Flt Engineer	POW
	Martin	Carter	12-Aug-1944	LM180	Russelsheim	Bomb Aimer	Evaded
)	John	Chapman	28-Jul-1944	LL692	Stuttgart	Bomb Aimer	Evaded
	Robert	Chester-Master	12-Aug-1944	LM180	Russelsheim	Rear Gunner	Evaded
)	James	Clare	21-Jan-1944	LL672	Magdeburg	Bomb Aimer	POW
t	John	Clarke	07-Jun-1944	DS822	Massy Palaiseau	Flt Engineer	POW
	F	Collingwood	07-Jun-1944	LL727	Massy Palaiseau	Flt Engineer	POW
	PG	Cooper	12-Jun-1944	DS818	Gelsenkirchen	Flt Engineer	POW
	HJ	Cosgrove	30-Mar-1944	LL696	Nuremburg	Navigator	POW
)	Argyle	Cunningham	11-May-1944	LL739	Louvain	Pilot	POW
t	SG	Cuttler	21-Jan-1944	LL672	Magdeburg	Navigator	POW
)	Harry	Darby	30-Mar-1944	DS836	Nuremburg	Bomb Aimer	POW
	Roger	Davis	20-Dec-1943	DS817	Frankfurt	Pilot	POW
)	Keith	Deans	22-Mar-1944	DS815	Frankfurt	Bomb Aimer	POW
	Francis	Dennehy	03-Aug-1944	LL716	Bois de Cassan	Mid Under Gunner	Evaded
t	William	Donaldson	28-Jul-1944	LL692	Stuttgart	Flt Engineer	Evaded
)	Derek	Duncliffe	12-Jun-1944	DS818	Gelsenkirchen	Pilot	Evaded
/O	Archibald	Durham	07-Jun-1944	DS822	Massy Palaiseau	Navigator	Evaded
t	EG	Durland	12-Aug-1944	LM180	Russelsheim	Wireless Op	Evaded
)	Frederick	Eisberg	21-Nov-1944	PD265	Homberg	Navigator	POW
t	WH	Ellis	21-Nov-1944	NG121	Homberg	Rear Gunner	POW
O	Maurice	Emery	02-Dec-1943	DS738	Berlin	Navigator	POW
/O2	William	Eyre	03-Aug-1944	LL716	Bois de Cassan	Rear Gunner	POW
t	GC	Fearman	22-Mar-1944	DS815	Frankfurt	Rear Gunner	Evaded

169

F/S	Ronald	Fox	07-Jun-1944	LL727	Massy Palaiseau	Navigator	E
F/O	Geoffrey	France	21-Nov-1944	PD265	Homberg	Pilot	Pe
Sgt	R	Galloway	02-Dec-1943	DS738	Berlin	MU Gunner	Pe
F/S	Earl	Garland	28-Jul-1944	LL692	Stuttgart	Navigator	Ev
F/S	H	Gilmore	03-Aug-1944	LL716	Bois de Cassan	Wireless Op	PC
Sgt	GF	Good	11-Sep-1944	DS787	Kamen	Flt Engineer	PC
F/O	Louis	Greenburgh	07-Jun-1944	LL727	Massy Palaiseau	Pilot	Ev
F/S	RL	Gulliford	30-Jan-1944	DS735	Berlin	2nd Pilot	PC
F/S	Bernard	Haines	18-Nov-1943	DS784	Mannheim	Rear Gunner	PC
F/S	AD	Hall	30-Mar-1944	LL738	Nuremburg	Bomb Aimer	PC
Sgt	Thomas	Harvell	28-Jul-1944	LM206	Stuttgart	Flt Engineer	Ev
F/S	Sam	Harvey	28-Jul-1944	LL692	Stuttgart	Rear Gunner	Ev
F/L	Guy	Hinde	02-Dec-1943	DS738	Berlin	Pilot	PC
Sgt	Percy	Hoare	22-Mar-1944	DS815	Frankfurt	Navigator	PO
Sgt	GM	Holt	12-Aug-1944	LM265	Russelsheim	Flt Engineer	PC
F/O	Peter	Hood	30-Mar-1944	LL696	Nuremburg	Pilot	PO
Sgt	Edward	Humes	11-Apr-1944	LL639	Aachen	Navigator	PO
F/S	Albert	Jackson	22-Mar-1944	DS815	Frankfurt	MU Gunner	Ev
F/S	Earl	Jones	28-Jul-1944	LL692	Stuttgart	MU Gunner	Eva
T/S	Maurice	Lanthier	30-Mar-1944	LL696	Nuremburg	Rear Gunner	PO
P/O	Lyndon	Lewis	07-Jun-1944	DS822	Massy Palaiseau	Bomb Aimer	PO
Sgt	HA	Lucas	18-Nov-1943	DS784	Mannheim	MU Gunner	Eva
Sgt	Arthur	Lyons	28-Jul-1944	LL692	Stuttgart	Wireless Op	Eva
F/S	CGE	MacDonald	30-Mar-1944	LL698	Nuremburg	Navigator	PO
Sgt	Gerald	Martin	12-Jun-1944	LL678	Gelsenkirchen	Flt Engineer	Eva
F/S	Ronald	McAllister	24-Mar-1944	LL625	Berlin	MU Gunner	PO
P/O	William	McGown	07-Jun-1944	DS822	Massy Palaiseau	Pilot	Eva
F/O	JR	McLenaghan	03-Aug-1944	LL716	Bois de Cassan	Bomb Aimer	PO
F/S	A	McPhee	30-Mar-1944	DS836	Nuremburg	Navigator	PO
F/O	WD	McPhee	22-Mar-1944	LL684	Frankfurt	Bomb Aimer	PO
F/S	Charles	Medland	21-May-1944	LL695	Duisburg	Pilot	PO
F/S	John	Moloney	24-Dec-1943	LL671	Berlin	MU Gunner	PO
Sgt	SW	Moore	02-Feb-1945	NN772	Wiesbaden	Bomb Aimer	PO
F/O	Arnold	Morrison	15-Jun-1944	DS816	Valenciennes	Navigator	Eva
F/S	Kenneth	Mortimer	30-Jan-1944	DS735	Berlin	Navigator	PO
Sgt	W	Muskett	02-Dec-1943	DS738	Berlin	Wireless Op	PO
F/L	Cyril	Nichol	22-Mar-1944	DS815	Frankfurt	Pilot	PO
F/S	Denison	Orth	12-Aug-1944	LM180	Russelsheim	Navigator	Eva

Lancasters at Waterbeach

George	Palamountain	12-Jun-1944	LL678	Gelsenkirchen	Bomb Aimer	Evaded
Robert	Ramsay	11-May-1944	LL739	Louvain	Navigator	POW
John	Reid	03-Aug-1944	LL716	Bois de Cassan	Flt Engineer	POW
Robert	Rigden	12-Sep-1944	LL731	Frankfurt	Bomb Aimer	POW
Eric	Rippingale	07-Jun-1944	LL727	Massy Palaiseau	Bomb Aimer	Evaded
Bleddyn	Roberts	11-May-1944	LL739	Louvain	Rear Gunner	Evaded
Alexander	Robertson	30-Jan-1944	DS735	Berlin	Rear Gunner	POW
Charles	Robinson	11-Sep-1944	DS787	Kamen	MU Gunner	POW
George	Robinson	28-Jul-1944	LM206	Stuttgart	Navigator	POW
Kenneth	Robinson	26-Aug-1944	LL728	Kiel	Bomb Aimer	POW
VJ	Rollings	30-Mar-1944	LL696	Nuremburg	Wireless Op	POW
J	Scully	03-Aug-1944	LL716	Bois de Cassan	MU Gunner	POW
L	Shimmons	21-May-1944	LL695	Duisburg	Wireless Op	Evaded
RC	Sime	22-Mar-1944	LL684	Frankfurt	MU Gunner	POW
Ronald	Smith	21-Jan-1944	LL672	Magdeburg	Wireless Op	POW
WJ	Stephen	02-Dec-1943	DS738	Berlin	Flt Engineer	POW
John	Stone	11-May-1944	LL739	Louvain	Wireless Op	Evaded
Leslie	Sutton	07-Jun-1944	LL727	Massy Palaiseau	2nd Pilot	Evaded
John	Topham	03-Aug-1944	LL716	Bois de Cassan	Pilot	Evaded
FC	Townshend	22-Mar-1944	DS815	Frankfurt	Flt Engineer	POW
Colin	Turner	12-Sep-1944	LL731	Frankfurt	Flt Engineer	POW
Leslie	Venus	21-May-1944	LL695	Duisburg	Bomb Aimer	POW
Victor	Vizer	21-Jan-1944	LL680	Magdeburg	Pilot	POW
Dennis	Walker	21-May-1944	LL695	Duisburg	Navigator	POW
EJ	Wallington	30-Jan-1944	DS735	Berlin	Bomb Aimer	POW
HH	Wickson	30-Mar-1944	LL696	Nuremburg	Flt Engineer	POW
Spurgeon	Williams	12-Jun-1944	LL678	Gelsenkirchen	MU Gunner	Evaded
Robert	Wilton	30-Mar-1944	LL696	Nuremburg	Bomb Aimer	POW
Donald	Winterford	11-May-1944	LL739	Louvain	Flt Engineer	POW
Richard	Woosnam	07-Jun-1944	LL727	Massy Palaiseau	Rear Gunner	POW
Tom	Young	12-Aug-1944	LM180	Russelsheim	Flt Engineer	Evaded

Comments on Bombing – The Author's View

I wish to comment on some aspects of bombing in WW2 as RAF bombing has been subjected to controversial criticism from time to time by sections of the media, possibly for sensationalistic gain. We seem to hear much about Dresden, where probably 30,000 people sadly died in a fire storm, but little else of the accomplishments of Bomber Command.

In truth RAF bombers significantly reduced Germany's ability to wage war efficiently. Apart from attacks on German cities they operated in many other areas including provision of invaluable support for the invasion in Normandy and following land battles. They destroyed six of Germany's twelve major warships and probably more than 75 U-boats and prevented the construction of as many more again. Air mining resulted in the sinking of over 700 ships plus over 600 damaged. Numerous industrial, communication, oil, missile and other specific targets were attacked, increasingly so as the war progressed. Due to the destruction being inflicted by RAF bombing, Germany needed to employ over a million men in defence and other related services. These men and the weaponry involved would otherwise have been available for the fighting fronts.

United States bombing in Europe was generally confined to industrial and military targets. Although they commenced with this policy against Japan, in order to bring the war to an earlier conclusion they switched to area bombing in March '45. Firstly Tokyo was attacked on the night of March 9th / 10th with fire-bombs, resulting in a fire storm and the death of over 80,000 people. Similar attacks followed on 60 other cities and towns culminating in the ultimate area bombing of Hiroshima and Nagasaki with atomic bombs.

Germany in WW2 was a tyranny of immense proportions. Hitler didn't attain power by the use of force but was elected into power by the German people. In the November 1932 elections the Nazis were again voted in as the largest party in the Reichstag leading to Hitler being offered the role of Chancellor, from which position it was relatively easy for him to acquire total dictatorial control. The German people knew, or should have known, what he was like before they voted; his hatred of the Jews, his expansionist aims in the east and his desire for revenge against France. This was all stated in his book Mein Kampf. The German electorate had let the evil genie out of the bottle and would live to regret it, along with most of Europe.

Following the fall of Poland and France Hitler was acclaimed by most of the population of Germany. His armies and other armed services, who fought for him with courage and skill, were supported and sustained by the German nation. Germany possessed the world's leading nuclear scientists and might well have been the first to produce the atomic bomb. They invented nerve gas against which there was no defence, but didn't use it in the mistaken belief that we had it also. They were inventive, well ahead of us in missile and rocket development. It was essential to strike at this resourceful and powerful enemy in any and every way and the only feasible way for Britain up to mid-1944 was by bombing at night. During this time all that could normally be targeted at night were areas of cities and towns, in which much of the power of Germany was concentrated.

Briefly they invaded and enslaved well over half of Europe and large areas of Russia, killing in the process at least 26 million people, including, amongst others, millions of persecuted and helpless Jews (men, women and children) who were put to death or died in their horror camps. Even while our crew was flying over Germany, from August to December '44, this process continued. Anne Franke, to name but one, was taken in September '44. I have no regrets that we took the war back to Germany where it belonged.

Following D Day in June '44 when areas of N France were being liberated and allied fighters had gained control of the skies over Germany by day, RAF bombers could have been, and possibly should have been at this stage of the war, used more frequently in daylight against military, industrial and other specific targets. Fortunately 514 Squadron, because of its specialist equipment, operated mainly in this role. The decision to permit Sir Arthur

Harris to resume the bombing of German cities alter the D Day Invasion period was a strategic decision and as such the responsibility of the War Cabinet and Defence Committee. London at this time was being indiscriminately bombarded by VI and V2 missiles.

With regard to the attack on Dresden in February '45 it should not be forgotten that Churchill himself for various reasons, was pressing for heavy attacks on certain eastern German cities including Dresden, which lay in the path of the advancing Russians. Any blame in the choice of targets in the later stages of the war rests solely with those at the highest levels of command. No blame can be placed on the aircrews nor any others in Bomber Command. The crews never questioned the targets they were sent to, trusting they were chosen by knowledgeable and wise counsels way above them. Despite heavy losses, they did all that was asked of them in the dangerous skies over Europe and should be proud that they took part in the destruction of perhaps the world's greatest tyranny. They also assisted in great measure in bringing freedom back to much of Europe including Germany itself which happily is now one of the world's great democracies.

OVER 55,000 DIED IN SERVICE WITH BOMBER COMMAND

Harry Dison

Lancasters at Waterbeach

30885250R00099

Printed in Great Britain
by Amazon